STRATEGIES FOR BAGGING
YOUR TROPHY BRUIN

SUCCESSFUL
BLACK BEAR
HUNTING

Text and Photos by
Bill Vaznis

©2004 by Bill Vaznis
Published by

 **kp krause publications**
An F+W Publications Company

700 East State Street • Iola, WI 54990-0001
715-445-2214 • 888-457-2873
www.krause.com

Our toll-free number to place an order or obtain
a free catalog is (800) 258-0929.

Library of Congress Catalog Number: 2004100331

ISBN: 0-87349-665-5

Designed by Brian Brogaard

Edited by Joel Marvin

Printed in China

About the Author

Bill Vaznis has pursued black bears throughout much of their range for the past 30 years. He is a full-time outdoor writer and wildlife photographer whose work has appeared in every major outdoor magazine in North America. He has published over 1000 feature articles and columns plus thousands of color and black and white photographs on bow-hunting, big-game hunting and freshwater fishing,

Bill Vaznis grew up in Northampton, Massachusetts. He graduated *cum laude* from the University of Massachusetts at Amherst and later earned an MSW from Tulane University Graduate School in New Orleans. He now lives in upstate New York.

Contents

Introduction

Some see the black bear as a frightening, blood-thirsty beast who kills purely for pleasure, while to others he is nothing more than a pest to be shot on sight. Still others, however, see him as a true symbol of the wilderness, and a fleeting glimpse of him becomes a life-long treasure. Whatever he is, one thing is for certain: Next to the whitetail deer, the American black bear is the most popular big-game animal on the continent.

Ironically perhaps, very little is known about *Ursus americanus*. His shy and secretive nature makes him quite difficult to study in his native habitat. Indeed, woods-wise sportsmen and women rate the black bear as one of the most elusive critters in the wild. A bear's eyes and ears can easily pinpoint danger, and his sense of smell is second to none. In fact, only the wolf is considered to be more difficult to catch flat-footed in the wild.

But there is another aspect to the black bear that hunters find fascinating and that is his intelligence. Unlike deer and elk that routinely flee from man, a black bear habitually challenges our intrusion into his world. If you happen to jump a big buck from a preferred feeding site, he'll probably vacate the area for several weeks. Push a bruin around, however, and he may very well be back by nightfall to steal your lunch. In fact, on rare occasions, he may even try to make you his lunch.

Indeed, the fear we all seem to have about black bears may be the most intriguing aspect of his character. For although we are probably more likely to get hit by lightning than attacked by a black bear, the fact that possibility exists makes him all the more challenging to hunt.

Trophy Bruins: Where Are They Hiding?

Tired of shooting 100-pound black bears?
Get off the beaten path—way off—and head into the big woods for record-book blackies!

mericans have been enthralled with black bears and bear hunting ever since Davy Crockett "killed hiself a bar when he was only three." Today, black bears are hunted in the spring and/or fall across most of Canada and many states in the lower 48. In fact, interest in big black bears has risen to the point where many knowledgeable hunters now claim that tagging a mature boar is as challenging as tagging a mature whitetail buck—maybe even more!

But where do you start? Bomber bears, like record-book bucks, don't grow on trees, and like record-book deer, you have to hunt where big bears live if you want to increase your chances of tagging a trophy-class bruin.

Keep in mind that most record-book bruins are older, mature males at least six years of age. In fact, there are no known female entries in the Boone and Crockett record books, and only a handful of the black bears listed in the Pope and Young record book are listed as "F".

A boar foraging for that many summers will often have an 18-inch skull, large enough to qualify for the archery or blackpowder record books. Occasionally, according to Alberta bear biologist John Gunson, a bear this age will also qualify for the Boone and Crockett record book. That said, the biggest black bears, those boars whose live weights push the scales to 400 pounds and beyond, generally prefer vast stretches of rugged wilderness or big woods areas adjacent to active farmland. The boreal forest and agricultural regions in southern Canada immediately come to mind, where low hunting pressure coupled with lengthy seasons and liberal bag limits make those provinces a hot spot for trophy bruins.

Please remember that this is just a guide to help get you started. A trophy black bear can come from almost anywhere bears reside, even in areas not noted for monster bruins. And be aware that regulations, even the ones I mention here, can vary from one state or province to the next. In fact, they can and sometimes do change from one season to the next, so always check with game officials before you step afield.

CANADA

Canada has hundreds of thousands of black bears, many of which will die without ever crossing paths with a human being. And although hunting techniques often vary from one province to the next, a serious hunter can often get a crack at a good spring or fall bruin with the weapon and method of choice by simply booking a hunt with a reputable outfitter.

If you live in New England or along the east coast, it's tough to beat Newfoundland, New Brunswick or Nova Scotia for big black bruins. Take Newfoundland for example. The historically low hunting pressure on the island—coupled with a population of 6000 to 10,000 bears—is reason enough to book a hunt, but it is the number of large bears that really gets my blood boiling. I have seen several spring bears there over 500 pounds, including one 675-725 pound specimen that still has my knees knocking. After a two-week wait, I watched it follow an estrous sow into the bait site, eat quickly and then leave hot on her tail without offering me an acceptable bow shot. And to the best of my knowledge, nobody ever saw that behemoth again!

These Newfoundland boars are so cunning and so ferocious that researchers have documentation proving mature boars can kill a full-grown bull moose with one swipe of a paw. I have also talked to several bush pilots who have seen bears from the air that they at first thought were

You have to hunt where big bears thrive to increase your chances of tagging a record-class bruin.

The biggest bears prefer vast stretches of rugged wilderness or big woods adjacent to active farmland.

This Quebec bear broke into our caribou camp on the Whale River and was shot by the outfitter. Few bruins this far north ever tip the 350-pound mark

feeding moose. I have no doubt that a 1000-plus pound giant bear will eventually be shot on the island, probably as a bonus kill by a non-resident moose hunter—or a patient bowhunter willing to wait one out over bait.

New Brunswick also has the potential to produce trophy bruins, especially in the north-central and southeastern regions. According to the third edition of *The Guinness Book of Animal Facts and Feats*, Joseph Allen killed a nightmare of a bruin near Millstream in 1976 after it killed his pet German shepherd. The bear measured seven feet eleven inches from nose to base of tail and tipped the

scales dressed at 902 pounds. Its live weight was later estimated to be 1100 pounds!

If there is a "sleeper" Canadian black bear hideout, it has to be Nova Scotia. Residents here have only recently caught "bear fever," and by all accounts, those afflicted have it bad. Some huge bruins have been tagged in recent years, including several in the 300 to 400-pound class on the west side of the province. I have no doubt though that lots of 600-plus pounders are still roaming around the thick forest, ripe for a close encounter. As an added bonus, Nova Scotia is one of the few places in the East where you might see a brown-phase blackie.

Hunting pressure is light in this tiny province, with less than 300 licenses sold annually, and only a couple of dozen of those are purchased by non-residents. I expect the numbers of big bears to remain good, at least for the time being. Why? There are no plans to open a spring season, and the fall hunt, which by law can take place only over a registered bait site, is usually over with by the time deer season opens. This makes it less likely an old boar will stumble into a deer hunter and become a target of opportunity.

East-coast bear hunters should not overlook Quebec for trophy bruins. The better bear hunting lies along the hardwood ridges in the middle of the province, and in the western regions along the Ontario border where, according to bear biologist Helene Jolicoeur, most of the prov-

The "bush" in Newfoundland, New Brunswick and Nova Scotia harbors gargantuan bruins.

ince's 60,000 bruins reside. This is where most of the really big bears thrive, too. (HINT: If you are seeing moose in Quebec, you are in prime bear country!)

There are also thousands and thousands of miles of wilderness shoreline here, making for excellent fishing too, especially if good-eating walleyes and toothsome northern pike are to your liking. In fact, it is not hard to find hundreds of miles of waterways here that you can have all to yourself—all the fixings for a great combo fishing and spring bear adventure.

Each year caribou hunters in northern Quebec stumble upon a big bear or two. Most bruins this far north are small by nature, but I did spot a 400-pounder from the air one fall on a return flight to Schefferville. The pilot banked the plane around for a second look-see, and we were all surprised at the amount of fat on this roly-poly bear. A small bear population and a bumper crop of blueberries in a wilderness setting will do that!

It is Ontario, however, that gets the nod for sheer numbers of trophy bears. In fact, only Colorado runs a distant second when it comes to entries in the various record books. Two reasons for this unparalleled success are a pool of good outfitters and a bear population of 75,000-100,000 animals. Only time will tell what effect the closing of the spring season will have on trophy hunting in Ontario, although I expect the ban to be eventually lifted.

Any place free of man is a good place to hunt bears in

The Saskatchewan River near Flin Flon, Manitoba, is teeming with 400-pound plus bruins in various color phases. The river restricts access to only the hardiest of hunters.

Ontario, and you can begin your search in mid-province near the Quebec border. In fact, I took my first bear not far from the Ottawa River nearly 30 years ago, and the fascination for these creatures has not diminished.

If you have your heart set on an off-color bruin, then set your sights on Manitoba, Saskatchewan or Alberta. Manitoba for instance has many good bears, and a quota system for non-resident licenses helps keep the hunting pressure light. There is also a one-bear limit. Trophy bears seem to be concentrated in the middle of the province

If you have your heart set on a color-phase bruin, then good outfitting is the key to success.

Don't overlook wooded areas near small towns for big bears. This Pennsylvania behemoth sauntered between fenced yards at will, looking for unattended bird feeders, garbage cans and, of course, handouts from local residents. No wonder he is so fat!

where fall specimens can weigh from 600 to 800 pounds. I like the Saskatchewan River area near Flin Flon the best.

To sweeten the "bait," one outfitter told me his harvest consists of 20 percent off-color bruins. Indeed, whenever there is an off-color bear around camp, it seems everybody wants a crack at him! Chocolate is probably the most common off-color followed by cinnamon, whereas bears with blond coats are considered much more rare.

Saskatchewan is also noted for its one-bear limit and

healthy population of blond-brown trophy-sized bruins. The real draw to this province, however, is the fact that archers have taken more Boone and Crockett bears here than in any other state or province. The big bears seem to come from areas that receive light hunting pressure, but good outfitting is one of the keys to success. Look for forested areas interfaced with natural and agricultural foods, or wilderness tracts that offer access but have not yet been hunted.

Alberta is one of my favorite places to hunt trophy bruins. It has good numbers of mature black and color-phase bears residing in both active farm country and untouched wilderness, and a two-bear limit. And best of all, the population is well managed.

Three-fourth's of the bruins reside in the forested northern half of the province where the bears are definitely big, but I've had my best luck in the fall, baiting near farmlands an hour or so north of Edmonton.

Indeed, I've successfully still-hunted mature boars with archery tackle in the broken farm country just north of Edmonton, and I've tagged several record-book blackies over bait in that area and in the wilderness north of Ft. McMurray. My heaviest Alberta bruin to date had a girth of 56 inches and an estimated live weight approaching 500 pounds. Alberta does have it all!

British Columbia, our western-most province on the big-bear trail, has a population estimated to be between

Maine has plenty of hunting opportunities if you are on a budget.

A bear-proof cabin located in Watson's Triangle, deep in New York's famed Adirondack Mountains. Notice the electric fence, powered by batteries storied in the back of the cabin. Built entirely by hand by M. C. "Mike" Vickler, his wife Hilda and a few friends, the camp was later dismantled and moved to The Adirondack Museum near Blue Mountain Lake where it is now on display. Watson's Triangle is now part of the Forest Preserve.

35,000 and 90,000 bruins, and as in much of Canada, this population is under harvested. Nonetheless, bowhunters have managed to put over 60 boars in the book over recent years—a very respectable figure!

The hottest bear hunting in the province right now is on Vancouver Island. Although many bruins are tagged by hunters after moose and caribou, most of the better bears are taken using the spot-and-stalk method. And although archers and modern rifle hunters are welcome, this country is really ideal for the blackpowder buff. Body weights between 300 and 500 pounds are not all that uncommon.

UNITED STATES

As you can see, Canada is crawling with big black bears. Some good bruins can also be found in the lower 48 states although short seasons and other restrictions make it difficult—but not impossible—for the average hunter to put a big bear or two into any one of the several record books. Here are some notable exceptions:

Pennsylvania's 15,000 black bears appear in nearly every county but are found predominantly in the northeast, north-central and south-central regions. The state's short, three-day season usually results in a dozen or so 600-pounders, taken mostly by drives and still-hunting. Dogs and baiting are not allowed.

Most sows here breed at 2.5 years of age and produce three to five cubs every two years. State officials claim the world's second largest black bear was poached within its borders, an 800-plus-pound giant that was eventually recovered and given a full body mount.

North Carolina has two distinct populations. There are 4000 bruins living in the Appalachians and about 7000 of the larger coastal bears, whose body weights have been recorded at just below 900 pounds, living along the Atlantic Ocean. The Piedmont, which lies between these two regions, is practically devoid of bears.

Females start breeding at 3 years of age, and males plateau out at about 450 pounds at 5 years of age. Winters are not as harsh here, thus they do not use as much of their fat reserves. In addition, they raid local farms, gorging themselves on such high-fat products as peanuts. Dog hunting is quite popular here; baiting is illegal.

Maine has more bear hunting opportunities for the average man. Most of the state's 23,000 bruins live east of the Penobscot River and north of Bangor.

Color-phase bears are very, very rare, and you usually have to weed through lots of subordinate bears before you cross paths with a record-class bruin. The good news is that in the better habitat, biologists tell us that all it takes is 4 to 5 years for a boar to grow an 18-inch skull and 6 to 8 years for

The midwestern states are also noted for black bears in the 300- to 400-pound range.

Biologist use a mix of barbed wire and genetics to gauge black bear populations. Outfitters and hunters will also use barbed wire to determine the color of bears hitting their baits.

a 21-inch skull. The bad news is that elsewhere, slow growth rates prohibit many mature bears from attaining record-book status. Fall baiting, dogs and trapping are all legal.

The sleeper in the northeast is undoubtedly New Hampshire. Five thousand black bears can be found throughout the state. A younger, expanding population lies in the southwest and southeast portions of the state, whereas bigger and more robust bruins tend to be found in the north-central segment, where males 5 to 10 years of age often reach substantial size. There is also plenty of access. Fall baiting and dogs are allowed, but trapping is forbidden.

For the do-it-yourself hunter, your chances are probably best in New York even though dogs and baiting are not legal. There are 5000 bears in the Adirondacks, and dressed weights of over 500 pounds are quite possible in Franklin, Essex, Hamilton and, to some degree, St. Lawrence counties. This is wilderness hunting at its best, where some bears reach 30 years of age, and a few are still padding about at 40. The most successful hunters scout out the mast crop year-round before concentrating their hunting efforts on those ridges and hollows that hold plenty of cherries early in the season and then beechnuts and acorns later on.

There are an additional 1000 or so bears in the rest of the state, mostly in the Catskills where archers have been catching some jumbo bruins in the over-600-pound class—dressed—raiding local cornfields. The nod goes to Delaware, Orange,

Sullivan and Ulster counties. A 4.75-year-old bruin here can occasionally tip the scales at 500 pounds.

Recently, a 6-month-old baby was killed by a black bear in the Catskills, the first reported human fatality in recent memory. It seems the bear, a 155-pounder, snatched a stroller holding the baby while adults were in attendance. A tug of war ensued, and the bear grabbed the baby by her head, killing her instantly. This bear was probably habituated to some degree to humans and was attracted to the baby's dirty diaper or formula. Whatever the circumstances, this proves once again that black bears are nothing to fool with—even the "small" ones.

MIDWEST

The upper Midwest is also home to substantial black bear populations. Minnesota, for example, has 25,000 to 30,000 bears residing primarily in the northern two-fifths of the state. A fair number of these bears are 5-year-old boars weighing 350 pounds on the pad, with bigger ones in the mix. Indeed, every year a 500-pound-class boar is tagged, with a 600-pounder taken about once a decade. Bear hunting during the regular deer season and hunting with dogs are not allowed, but hunting over bait is quite popular.

In 2002, Minnesota reported its second bear attack on a human in 30 years. The victim was a grouse researcher who stumbled upon the bruin while doing field study. He

Most book bears are mature males. However, the very oldest bears are more likely to be female.

Spot-and-stalk is popular in our western states. Ten power binoculars are standard equipment.

fought back, as you are supposed to do with a black bear, but to no avail. When the researcher played dead, however, as you are supposed to do when dealing with a grizzly, the bruin wandered off. Dogs were brought in in hopes of killing the renegade bear, but the trail was too cold. The bear has not been seen since.

Some pertinent facts that should be of interest to any serious bear hunter emerge from bear harvest data in this state. The annual bear kill, for example, fluctuates wildly from one year to the next. Why? It seems the more natural food available during the fall hunting season, the lower the bear kill, and conversely, the less natural food available, the higher the bear harvest.

The age of male bears in the annual harvest is also significant. According to Minnesota harvest figures, the average male tagged is only 2.5 years of age while the average female tagged is about 4 years old. Why aren't more of the state's older mature boars tagged? Well, according to state officials, every year experienced bear hunters wait for these old boars to make a showing at a bait site. But old bears are smart bears, and they are more likely than a younger bear to wait for the hunter to return to camp at dark before hitting the bait. Thus, younger bears are more likely to be shot.

The age of some males may not be accurately reported either, especially when the bear's age is recorded to be over 35 years of age. According to bear biologist Dave Garshelis, "most bears, be they black bear or grizzly, rarely live past their mid-thirties in the wild. How can a mistake be made? During the breeding season, boars fast for two to three weeks. This can give them an extra 'line' in their tooth called a 'summer line'. If this faint extra line is not taken into account by the lab, a big boar can gain two years on paper for every year it actually ages.

"Secondly, we have also radio-collared many bruins over the years. Before we return the bear to the wild, we record such vital statistics as weight and sex. If a hunter tags a radio-collared bear, they are asked to report the kill to officials. About 10 percent of the hunters misidentify the sex of the bear, either by error, which can be understandable given the size of a bear's sex organs, or because of the hunter's ego. It seems no one wants to admit they shot a sow. Real men it seems shoot boars, and big ones at that!"

Although, as mentioned earlier, most book bears are mature males, the very oldest bears are more likely to be females. And when you think about it a bit, it makes sense. Females tend to live longer in part because their home ranges are smaller, and they are less likely to be shot by a

Rugged terrain keeps most bear hunters at bay. You'll need horses to hunt the better sections.

hunter. They, like the females of many species including man, also seem to age at a slower rate than males.

Males, on the other hand, do not live longer in the wild in part because their ranges generally overlap several female territories, they have a bolder temperament and they are more likely to be shot by a hunter.

The western reaches of Michigan's Upper Peninsula are also noted for their black bear habitat. Baiting and dogs are legal, as is spot-and-stalk, but due to the thick habitat, less than 5 percent of licensed hunters practice the latter.

Although 500-pounders are tagged here, the bears in general are not as big as they are in Pennsylvania or North Carolina. This is due in part to the younger age structure. The majority of the bruins are young, averaging 3 years of age even, though bears as old as 35 years have been tagged here and every season a 15 to 25-year-old bear is shot. The onset of breeding is 4.5 years, whereas breeding begins at 2.5 years in the Lower Peninsula, a reflection of better food.

Interestingly, biologists employ a mix of barbed wire and genetics to gauge black bear populations in the state. "It is a tool that has been successfully used in some areas on grizzly bears," says bear biologist Dwayne Etter, "but also on black bears in Florida and New Jersey. During the summer, we start by setting up several bait stations in good areas known to harbor lots of bears. As soon as we start getting hits, we lace the entrance and exit trails with strands of barbed wire. As the bears move in to feed, they inadvertently leave strands of fur on the barbs. The samples collected are later compared to those from

harvested bears, giving us a more accurate picture of our black bear population. It is a lot easier to get the information we want this way than by the use of wire snares. A bear caught in a snare is nothing to fool with!"

Although Michigan and Minnesota are both represented in the various record-keeping organizations, the state of Wisconsin dominates the record-book scene in the Midwest. Why so many book bears in Wisconsin? Firstly, the population is well managed. Each year, about 5000 permits are awarded from a pool of 45-50,000 applicants, and, of these, 1800 to 2300 permit holders are successful. Secondly, there is a bona fide interest in bears and bear hunting, as evidenced by both a well-organized statewide bear hunting association and an ethical outfitter's association. Those hunters lucky enough to draw a permit are often contacted by mail by members of the outfitter's association. Booking with a professional bear hunter generally increases your chances of success. Finally, there is also a pool of hunters who are quite selective in their harvest, holding out for a real jumbo bear. Indeed, once you have one or two "average" bears under your belt, the adrenaline starts to flow for a big mature boar.

According to Kyle LaFond, there are nearly 12,000 bruins residing primarily in those forested regions located in the northern one-third of the state. Boars 5 to 6 years of age are common here and a good portion of these qualifies for one of the various record books. Several bears also tip the scales at 500 pounds each fall.

There is no spring hunt, but baiting and dogs are legal. The biggest bears seem to come from baited

Black bear populations have never been as high as they are now.

operations, but dogs take their fair share, too. Each year, several bruins 17 to 24 years of age are also tagged.

WESTERN UNITED STATES

The western states have gads of big bears. Indeed, Alaska, Idaho, Montana, California, Arizona, Utah, Washington, Oregon, Wyoming, New Mexico and Colorado all report gargantuan bruins within their borders, but the first five states mentioned seem to get the most attention.

In Alaska, black bears are becoming more popular targets with bowhunters, especially in the Prince of Wales and Quiu Island areas in the southeast. The best times to hunt are the first two weeks in May. This is really an untapped source of trophy black bears, but cost and distance seem to work against outfitters in the region. It is just too far and too expensive for the average eastern or mid-western bear hunter to travel for big bruins.

Idaho does not give out population estimates, but most biologists will tell you they believe 20,000 to 30,000 bruins inhabit their state, with the bulk of those found in the north and north-central regions. Baiting and dog hunting are both legal here, but spot-and-stalk with either rifle or bow is also popular when the berries are sugar sweet. Seven-foot black bears weighing 300 to 340 pounds are tagged every spring, and that means 400 to 500 pounders are available in the fall to those who want to put in their time.

Although the oldest black bear on record—a purported 35- or 36-year-old boar—was tagged recently near Yellowstone, the bulk of the Montana harvest is taken west of the continental divide. Baiting and dogs are illegal throughout the state, making the mountains and clearcuts a rifleman's paradise. The bears are not as big here as they are in Wisconsin, Pennsylvania or eastern Canada, at least by harvest data, but that does not mean there are not some real jumbos in the high backcountry. Indeed, most bear hunters shoot the first bear they see and have no idea how big it is until they poke it with the gun barrel. I suspect the older bears go unscathed in part because they are not specifically targeted by most bear hunters. The average bear harvested is 3 years old.

There are plenty of bruins in the south and southwestern sections of the state, but my favorite bear country has been in the northwest along the Yaak drainage system. In the fall when the berries are the sweetest, bears will gorge themselves on the huckleberry crop, and if you can be at the head of a hidden basin somewhere in the high country at dawn, your chances of connecting with a trophy bruin are actually quite good.

You should be aware that this is also grizzly country. Black bears lead a tenacious life here as they are pressured in both time and place around good feeding areas by the more aggressive grizzly—and for good reason. Although a big black bear boar will eat a grizzly cub or two given the opportunity, it is usually the other way around. In fact, if the literature is accurate, even a big mature blackie has reason to shy away from a marauding grizzly bear. Black bears taste good to a big griz!

If there is a sleeper in the West, then California gets the nod with its relatively unknown population of 25,000 to 35,000 bruins. According to bear biologist Doug Updike, 600-pound bears have been tagged just north of the Los Angeles basin as well as in the northern one-third of the state.

Big bears also reside up and down the mountainous spine of the Sierra Nevadas on the eastern side of the state. He believes the genetics to produce trophy bears are in these areas. Indeed, a bear's skeleton stops growing around 10 years of age. A bear is as big as he is going to be then, and with good nutrition and the right genes, he could turn out to be one very big scary bear.

The median age at harvest is around 5 to 6 years of age, which seems to indicate a lot of older males in the population. The oldest bruin tagged in the state was 32 years old, and bears in their 20s are regularly killed. The oldest bear in captivity, however, lived an amazing 44 summers. Dogs and those who like to spot-and-stalk account for the bulk of the kills. Baiting is not legal.

One look at the Boone & Crockett record book and you will see that the top 20 entries are loaded with Arizona bears. The odd part about these figures is that Arizona only has at best about 3000 black bears, and of those, only about 325 are tagged annually. Why so many world-class bruins from a state with such a small resident population of black bears? According to biologist Brian Wakeling, the answer is three fold. "First, most of our bears reside south of the Mogollon Rim. We have a lot of diversity among our big-game animals here, and those animals, including elk, pronghorn and black bear, are known for their better-than-average size. Secondly, we take a conservative approach to our harvest and that leaves room for older age animals to flourish. Finally, our hunters, both resident and non-resident, know that we have a trophy population of black bears and thus are more likely to hold out for a record-book animal."

If you think about that for a while, you will realize that Arizona's game management system holds the key to taking trophy black bears anywhere in their range. That is, you hunt where bigger bears are known to reside, in a state or province that tightly controls the harvest, and then you resist shooting immature specimens, holding out instead for a mature bear—the black bear of your dreams.

Mmm…Mr. Grizzly likes his black bear steaks on the rare side!

HOW MANY BLACK BEARS ARE OUT THERE?

Knowing approximately how many bears reside in any one state or province is both an art and a science. Although black bear populations are relatively stable from one year to the next, professional biologists do not always agree on an official figure. There are just too many unknowns with which to contend! Nonetheless, here are the latest general population figures, coupled with some average yearly harvest figures, for you to ponder.

STATE /PROVINCE	BLACK BEAR POPULATION	AVG. HARVEST
Alaska	100,000	2500
Arizona	2500-3000	325
Arkansas	3500	limited
California	23,000-35,000	1800
Colorado	9000-10000	725
Georgia	2000	300
Idaho	unknown	1,850
Maine	23,000	4000
Massachusetts	1800	80
Michigan	16,000	2200
Minnesota	20,000- 30,000	2000-5000
Montana	10,000-20,000	1000-1500
New Hampshire	5000	450
New Mexico	5500-6000	330
New York	5000-6000	750
North Carolina	10,000	1500
Oregon	25,000-30,000	950
Pennsylvania	15,000	3000
South Carolina	300	limited
Tennessee	2000	125
Utah	3000	90
Vermont	3300	425
Virginia	5000-6000	1000
Washington	30,000	1100
West Virginia	10,000	1300
Wisconsin	11,500	2200
Wyoming	unknown	200

Alberta	35,000	3000
British Columbia	35,000-90,000	4300
Manitoba	25,000-30,000	1800
New Brunswick	16,000	1900
Newfoundland /Labrador	8000-10,000	unknown
Nova Scotia	8500	225
Ontario	75,000-100,000	6750
Quebec	60,000	3800
Saskatchewan	30,000	2000
Yukon	7000	not reported

WORLD RECORD BEAR

The biggest bear ever taken by a human hunter is, unfortunately, not listed in any of the record books in part because the skull has never been officially measured. Score aside, we can pretty much guess what the bruin weighed by some of his bones left behind.

What kind of bear was he? Well, it was not a black bear, where a large boar will weigh 300 to 400 pounds, stand 30 to 36 inches at the shoulder and measure over 6.5 feet in length. This kind of bear is not big enough to take the crown, although I have no doubt a 1000 to 1100-pound behemoth will eventually be tagged in Pennsylvania or on the island of Newfoundland.

No, the world record bear was not a grizzly either. A big boar grizzly will weigh around 800 pounds, although there are enough long-claws in the 1000-pounds-and-above bracket alive today to make you think twice about spending the night alone next to a moose kill. Even so, a big grizzly will only stand 3.5 feet high at his humped shoulder and measure 7.5 feet in length.

No, the world record bear was not a polar bear. These critters can easily exceed 1000 pounds, with bears up to 2200 pounds recorded. These flesh eaters stand about 4 feet at the shoulder and measure 8 feet in length. While big—very big actually—this bear is also not big enough to make the claim of being the King of the Bears.

Sorry, the biggest bear ever brought down by a hunter was not a brown bear. Most trophy male browns weigh 800 to 1200 pounds, stand 4.5 feet at the shoulder and, when standing erect, might measure 9 feet in height. With front legs outstretched, an adult male can easily spread his paws 10 or 11 feet. Very impressive, indeed, but not anywhere near as impressive as the World Record.

No, the biggest bear ever killed by a hunter was much, much bigger.

This bear, and others of his kind, once lived in Pennsylvania, Indiana, Kentucky as well as California, northern Mexico and the Yukon. *Arctodus Simus*, the short-faced bear, stood on average 5 to 6 feet at the shoulder when on all fours and 12 to 14 feet when erect. He also had a 9-foot arm span. A so-so male probably weighed around 2000 to 2500 pounds!

As you may have guessed, the short-faced bear is now considered extinct. Five to ten thousand years ago, North American hunters did hunt him, however (and no doubt vice versa), as evidenced by cut marks from a Clovis Paleoindian spear point found on his bones.

But think about this. If the population of short-faced bears was similar to other populations of bears, then there were some individuals who grew to be twice the size of the average. This would make the biggest bears of this species push the scales over 5000 pounds and stand in excess of 20 feet tall!

And get this. There are a few researchers who think a small population of short-faced bears may still exist in Russia. Think about that the next time you're sitting 15 feet up in a tree and hear a twig snap behind you in the dark!

Now, in case you think I've been eating too many of my meals at bait stations, click on to www.cryptozoology.com and read "Bergman's Bear" by Andrew W. Gable. He tells of Sten Bergman, a Swedish zoologist, who in 1920 saw the pelt of an exceptionally large bear taken near the shore of the Bearing Sea in Kamchatka (Russia). The hair was unusually short for bears of that region and deep black in color. The tracks were of equal interest to Bergman. They measured 14.5 inches by 10 inches, indicating a truly giant animal. Bergman named the bear *Ursus arctos piscator*, but it is more commonly been called "Bergman's Bear." No sightings of the bear have been reported since 1936.

In the 1980s, however, reports came in from the region of a bear with long forelegs—far longer than the hind legs—and a bulge of fat between the hind legs that often reached the ground. The natives called the bear Irkuiem ("trousers pulled down") because of his appearance.

N.K. Vereshchagin, a Russian biologist who heard about the bear, theorized that Irkuiem was a surviving remnant of *Arctodus Simus*, "a bear that stood nearly six feet at the shoulders and was twice as large as the largest ursine when it reared up on its hind legs." His article appeared in a 1987 issue of *Ohota*.

Other researches vehemently disagreed with Vereshchagin, but with no hard evidence to support either claim, including that of Bergman, at least one question remains. Is Irkuiem really Bergman's Bear, or does *Arctodus Simus* still roam the wilds of Kamchatkan, Russia?

Choosing the Right Outfitter

Do you have your heart set on a trophy bruin? Then book with a specialist!

Our suspicions were confirmed. At first I thought it was a moose feeding on lily pads, but then the body of a large black bear, which must have been chasing beavers around in the backwater, shuffled into view 40 yards off to my right. He passed behind the stand, and then disappeared into the shadows.

A half-hour before dark, the boar reappeared, circling the bait and sniffing the air for signs of danger. Once he was satisfied all was safe, he committed himself to the set-up, but when he reached the cribbed offering, he suddenly jerked his head around and looked right at me.

The 400-pound bruin didn't lower his head one inch as he closed the distance between us. He quickly climbed a log, stood up on his hind legs and looked up at me with those beady brown eyes of his. Then he woofed—twice. I hid behind my Pro Revolution TRS as best I could and tried to stop from shaking.

If I could have taken one step away from the tree and raised my Golden Eagle over my head, I know I could have cold-cocked that old boar right then and there. Instead, I held my cool. When the bear returned to the bait site and turned broadside, I picked a spot low and behind his shoulder, slowly came to full draw and released a 2514 camo shaft fitted with a 100-grain Satellite TNT at his vitals.

The Pope & Young bruin immediately jumped the crib but then stopped and turned around as if to return to the bait. I thought I had missed, but then the boar took a few steps forward and fell over dead, traveling less than 10 yards from where I had shot him. The big bear never knew what hit him.

If you have your heart set on a trophy bear, you must go where the biggest males abound and then book with an outfitter who specializes in the 400-plus-pound specimens. And as discussed earlier, the Northeast, East, Midwest, Far West and all of southern Canada are crawling with gargantuan bruins. Your task now is to pick a location or two and start singling out outfitters who share your goals. Price is often a good indicator in this regard so expect to pay at least $1800 to $2000 or more for a quality hunt. You can book a cheaper hunt, but you may only get a horseback ride into the mountains or a bag of donuts tossed unceremoniously behind your cabin.

So how do you go about compiling a list of potential outfitters? One way is to use the services of a booking agent. Contrary to what some hunters may believe, it is the outfitter who pays the booking agent for his services, not the prospective hunter. In fact, the cost of using a booking agent is often already factored into the cost of the hunt, whether you use his services or not!

In other words, when you book through a qualified booking agent, the outfitter pays the booking agent a fee, usually 10 to 15 percent of the cost of the hunt (i.e. the price the outfitter is charging you to hunt with him). A $2000 bear hunt, for example, will earn the booking agent $200 to $300. The hunt is still going to cost you $2000 however.

Jeff Grab, co-owner of NorthCountry Expeditions, a booking agency headquartered in Stowe, Vermont, which

Serious outfitters prefer serious hunters as their clients and vice versa!

Caught off guard, a black bear will sometimes sit or stand up to better assess the situation.

I have used several times over the years, works hard to find his clients top-notch bear outfitters. "We will not recommend a bear camp to one of our customers," says Grab, "without first hunting from the camp ourselves. This gives us valuable insight into how the camp is run. There is a lot more to hunting bears than being able to produce trophies for anxious hunters. We also want to know, for example, how well trained are the guides, the quality of food, how well he keeps his equipment maintained and how he handles problems in camp such as excessive alcohol and rowdy hunters. These are all factors into making a hunt a successful trip and a memorable one for our clients.

"As the years pass we keep tabs on everything from bear harvests to the personal problems of the outfitter," adds Grab. "One outfitter, for example, went through an ugly divorce, which had a negative impact on the camp and the quality of the hunt. We waited until the outfitter had time to put his personal life back together again before we resumed booking for him. This was for the benefit of our customers as well as the reputation of the outfitter.

"Bear harvests are also important," adds Grab. "If success rates drop, it could indicate the outfitter is no longer doing his job. It could also mean, however, that the weather was a factor during the hunt or that the hunters were more interested in partying than hunting. Of course, that season's hunters may have been inexperienced and tended to freeze up when a bruin walked into range, or just the opposite. A camp full of experienced trophy hunters will pass up small-to-medium-sized bears for the chance at a real jumbo. These issues all have to be sorted out before we can book hunters for the following season."

A red flag goes up for me when an outfitter has numerous small females in his harvest reports and only a few large males taken over the last 3 or 4 years. This is a problem often associated with those outfitters who take in scores of hunters each season to help pay for a beautiful

Good booking agents visit bear camps regularly and then keep tabs on success rates, boar-to-sow ratios and any changes that might affect the outcome of your hunt.

Eric Grinnell of Silvertip Outfitters with a client's 400-pound book boar.

lodge. Contrary to what you might think, big boars are usually the first to be killed in any hunting area partly because their territories overlap that of several females. They also roam about more, and are thus more likely to come into contact with humans. Finally, big boars are also bolder, and will take over a food site, be it natural or man-made, by scaring off females and subordinate boars that may have discovered the cache of food first. Thus, a camp whose hunters consistently seem to tag only small females is more often than not a camp that has over-hunted its territory. The outfitter will have to move his hunting operation to a new sector if he wants to regain his reputation for bagging big bears.

Booking a black bear hunt on the advice of a friend or colleague can also save you a lot of headaches. A lot of questions about the camp, for example, can be answered truthfully and in private by someone you trust. How many bears did you see? How big were they? Did you get any shots? How were the guides? How was the fishing? How was the food? Did you sleep in tents? Is there a shower? Flush toilets? How bad were the bugs? Should I bring my own firearm as a backup? Do the guides do the skinning? How do I get my bear home? How did you get the meat home? How much money did you leave as a tip? Were there any hidden costs? Would you hunt with the outfitter again?

What you won't get is a biological report of the area and an unbiased forecast for the upcoming season. A call to the local big-game biologist might help (I have never had a conversation with a bear biologist where I didn't learn something!), but he probably won't play favorites among outfitters and he certainly won't tell you where a specific big bear is lurking.

Even when recommended by a close friend, an unscrupulous outfitter can still take advantage. For example, I had one outfitter tell me he would allow only so many hunters in camp to score. "Why should everyone return with a bear? If two guys out of four or five tag a bear—they will ALL be back next year, and probably with a few more clients. That means less work for my staff, and more bears in my zone!"

And if you're thinking it's too difficult for an outfitter to actually limit his kill in such a manner, think again. Frankly, it is quite easy to do, even when dealing with experienced bear hunters. Rifle hunters can be led to the "lost valley," where bears are as common as fur buyers at a PETA convention. And bowhunters can sit for days over a bait that appears to be visited regularly—but as it turns out, only by a nocturnal bear. Indeed, many large camps have such a bait set aside just for loudmouths, egomaniacs, know-it-alls—and the odd man out in a three- or four-man hunting party.

Of course, you can also book a hunt by attending outdoor shows or by responding to ads in the back of quality

Good news travels fast around a campfire.

outdoor magazines. I've met some outstanding outfitters in this manner and have had some great hunts. There is a word of caution, however, for you can also book the hunt from hell if you are not careful.

One outfitter, for instance, had a scrapbook full of "hero" shots of hunters with huge bears. I was curious and took a careful look at all the photos. As I suspected, not all the hunters pictured were his clients. One photo in particular was of a friend of mine with a bruin he had bagged with a different outfitter. Apparently, my buddy gave this outfitter the "hero shot" one night at a local watering hole. Had I not suspected something was amiss, I probably would not have studied the photo album so carefully.

Another outfitter claimed one of his clients took a huge bear mounted in his booth. It was an impressive bear, and many potential clients stopped by the booth to ogle the beast. As it turned out, the bear was not his and it did not come from the outfitter's concession. In fact, it did not even come from the same province.

QUESTIONS, QUESTIONS AND MORE QUESTIONS

After having been burned several times over the years by guides and outfitters who should be hung by their, ah, ankles, I've come up with a list of questions to ask an outfitter. They don't cover all the bases, but these questions are a good starting point. In the end, any outfitter that leaves you feeling uneasy is one to avoid while any outfitter who is not defensive and sounds knowledgeable is probably one worth exploring further.

Let's start with spot-and-stalk hunts. They can be physically demanding, so ask enough questions to insure you and your equipment are up to the task. How rough is the terrain and what elevation will you be hunting? If you are a "flatlander," any trip above 8000 feet may leave you dizzy and short of breath for a few days. Will you be on foot every day or will 4x4s be available? What about horses or mules? If either will be used, how many days do you expect to be in the saddle and how many hours a day? Unless you are already a horseman, you will want to do some riding before you arrive in camp. It usually takes a few days to get your knees, ankles and "tailbone" in shape. What style of boot does he recommend you wear, both for climbing and horseback riding? Will there be a need for any specialized clothing?

What is the game plan if inclement weather sets in? What is his definition of a trophy bruin? What is the upper end in bear size? What will the bears likely be feeding on when you are in camp? Are there grizzlies in the area? How many bears can you expect to see during your hunt? How many of these will be "shooters" and how many of those will be approachable? What caliber(s) does he recommend? What will be the longest shot he would expect you to tackle? Will you be shooting at odd or steep angles?

Even when recommended by a close friend, the bear hunt of a lifetime can quickly turn into the bear hunt from hell. Here, hunters have to repair a bridge before they can get their 4x4s into black bear country.

Should you bring shooting sticks? What power binocular does he recommend? If you are an eastern deep-woods deer hunter, would a range finder be helpful when estimating shooting distances over wide-open terrain?

For bowhunters, there is nothing like a baited hunt to increase your odds of success. But just because you book a bear hunt over bait does not insure you will tag a bruin. In fact, you may not even see a bear. It is just too easy for a fly-by-night outfitter to throw some meat scraps into a few piles along an old logging road and say he is running a bait line for trophy bears. As I said earlier, cost is often an indication of quality in this regard. Here is how I begin to weed out the good outfitters from the wannabes.

How long has he been baiting the area? The best camps are new and set up in virgin territory by outfitters with considerable bear-hunting experience. If the number of big boars harvested has dwindled significantly over the years, the area has probably been over-hunted.

Are the treestands permanent towers? Big bears are very, very smart and learn rather quickly to avoid these sites or only visit them under the cover of darkness. If the outfitter books 50 hunters a season, you can bet the big old boars are quite leery around these stands.

How many baits are available? I prefer to have a half-dozen or so bait sites to inspect when I arrive in camp; a dozen is even better. Not every site will attract

a trophy boar, and although all the baits might be "hit," there's no use sitting over one that isn't likely to produce a real jumbo. If the outfitter won't let you pick and choose to some extent, and you want a trophy bruin, then book with someone else.

What does he use for bait? I've hunted with five-star outfitters who used dated meat products, popcorn, donuts and barrels of wheat and oats rolled in molasses, and each one had bears galore visiting their sites regularly.

Whenever I have run my own bait line or hired a guide to start one 2 to 3 weeks before I was scheduled to arrive in camp, I've always had my best luck by starting out with a stink or "attractor" bait of rotting meat. Road kill stuffed in a large covered bucket left out in the sun for a couple of weeks works great. To get maximum "coverage," simply hang the bucket high and out of reach in a nearby tree. The morning and evening breezes will soon bring in the bears. In a pinch, you can also saturate a burlap bag with molasses or honey and hang the bag between a couple of branches.

As for the main offering, I've never been too excited about using dead fish, preferring instead to use fresh meat scraps laced with dated pastries to bring bears back again and again. Dead beavers, supplied by local trappers, will also do the trick. You can later fine-tune the main offering to the likes and dislikes of the visiting bears by adding

Successful bear camps are run and operated by knowledgeable outfitters and guides who attend to even the smallest of details.

more of what they like and eliminating that which they refuse to eat.

Volume is the real secret, however, to establishing a hot bait site. A small bag of meat scraps hung on a limb will in no way attract as many bears as a wheelbarrow full of different goodies. Rarely is there a bait site that is too big!

How far are the bait sites from one another? Each site should be at least a mile to 1.5 miles apart. If they are much closer, one bear can hit several baits in one evening, leading you to think the area is crawling with them.

How often are the baits checked? Some outfitters use 55-gallon barrels and don't have to replenish the bait site more than once or twice a week. Others, however, need more attention. There are two issues here. If baited regularly, bears can become accustomed to the baiting operation and react accordingly. That is, they will hit the bait soon after it has been replenished and not in the evening when you are likely to be waiting in ambush. This behavior is not insurmountable, however, and as we will discuss later, there are things you can do to tag such a bear.

The other issue is neglect. I hunted with one clown in Ontario who hung bags of dry dog food from tree limbs and then left it there without checking them until we showed up in camp 2 weeks later. He told us, with a loud voice and lots of finger pointing, to stay away from the bait so as not to "contaminate" it. After dinner that evening, he added,

"there's good bears on all the baits, so just be patient." The set-up sounded odd to us, and with a conspicuous absence of tracks and dung, we soon tore the baits apart. That's how we found that the bait sites, and the outfitter, were duds. We immediately cancelled our 2-week hunt and warned the next group of hunters to stay home.

Another bear outfitter also told us to stay away from the barrels, which he had covered in brush. After a couple of days of no-shows, we smelled a rat and removed the brush. The barrels were empty except for a few breadcrumbs. This bum had the gall to toss a loaf of bread into each barrel and then expect it to draw bears. The birds and red squirrels had a feast, but we weren't after these critters. This guy knew better, too!

We thought about dumping the camp, but instead I drove into town, located a meat processor and filled my 4x4 with meat scraps. It was too little, and too late, but a few average bears were tagged nonetheless. In retrospect, it would have been wiser to go home, file a complaint with the authorities and stop payment on all the checks.

Running a bait line is tough work, and if the outfitter is not going to periodically replenish the bait and otherwise keep tabs on the site, then your hunt will suffer. If the outfitter won't let you go on a bait run or otherwise tells you to stay away from the bait pile, then don't book with him.

You may find out the outfitter is hard working and

Ask a lot of questions if you are considering a spot-and-stalk hunt. And if you have never ridden a horse, it's best to get some experience beforehand. Ankles, knees and "tail" bones get a work out!

comes with good references, but what does he know about setting up treestands for bowhunters? Twelve to 15-yard shots from a well-hidden stand 10 to 12 feet off the ground is ideal. There should also be a portable stand or two in camp to help you deal with an exceptionally intelligent bruin.

Does he have provisions for acquiring blackpowder or its equivalent, especially when it is illegal to put any type of explosive device on a plane? How far are the stands from the bait site? Are the bait sites cribbed?

Finally, does he hunt himself, or is this just a hobby for him? The best outfitters are avid hunters themselves, but that does not mean the outfitter-hunter will be guiding you. After all, he has a camp to run, and there are myriad chores to be done to insure your trip is successful.

As you can see, there are many questions you can ask a potential outfitter to help you book that coveted "hunt of a lifetime." Even with a top-notch outfitter, however, you can still come home empty-handed. Weather is always a primary factor, as are your own hunting and shooting skills. But sometimes the fault lies with you. That's right, most hunters are their own worst enemies when it comes to punching a tag.

VARSITY BLUES

Well, you've finally booked the hunt of your dreams. You tell your friends all the details and even buy some new equipment. You can't wait to set your sights on a trophy black bear. So whose fault is it when you return home empty-handed?

"Ever hear about the House of Excuses?" my uncle asked me one day when I was a teenager. Before I could tell him that I had not, he informed me, rather smugly, that it had never been built, and if I ever wanted to amount to anything, I had to stop blaming others and take responsibility for my actions. "It is the only way a man can take charge of his life," he told me. It was good advice back then, and it is still good advice today.

Unfortunately, the affliction is still with us. Visiting local pro shops, I hear story after story how local bowhunters failed to fill a tag because the outfitter was a bum or someone else in camp got preferential treatment. Rarely do I hear that the real reason they failed to fill a tag was their own ineptitude.

Sure, you can book with a criminal outfitter and camp jealousies can just about ruin a trip. Even the weather can turn against you. And if that is not enough to contend with, sometimes the four-legged critters we chase simply outsmart us. That is, after all, why we call it hunting and not shopping! Nonetheless, there are times when we seem to be our own worst enemies when we are afield with bow, muzzleloader or modern firearm. What follows are five reasons—not excuses—why we sometimes fail to fill a tag:

If you are looking for a jumbo bruin, the best bear camps are set up in virgin territory.

1. DON'T GUIDE THE GUIDE

I love this one. Why bear hunters book hunts in Canada or out West or anyplace else for that matter and then show up in camp thinking they know it all is beyond me. Guys like this are going to do it their way because, after all, they are experts back home on hogs or whitetails or whatever. (And if he isn't a bonafide hero himself, someone in his family or circle of friends is!)

Nine times out of 10, however, these guys have never even seen a black bear in the wild and don't have the foggiest idea how to find one, much less set up for a shot. But instead of listening to the advice of the expert they hired, they blunder ahead without a clue of what to do.

One bear camp I shared illustrates this point splendidly. "Jimmy" had never hunted black bears before, but he was a top 3-D shot back east—at least that is what he told us—and somehow this made him an expert black bear hunter. He wasn't about to take a back seat to any "hillbilly" guide, and no one was going to tell him which bait he should hunt.

Well, on the third night out, there was a change in wind direction, and "Jimmy" was advised to hunt a bait station along a small creek. This bait had only been hit once in the last 4 days, but the guide was sure a bruiser of a bear was in the vicinity. "Jimmy," however, wanted to hunt a different site, the clear-cut bait, because it was being hit nightly. The guide told "Jimmy" that the clear-cut bait was being demolished regularly by a sow with twin cubs, but "Jimmy" insisted he was right and that the guide was an idiot.

Well, my buddy sat on that creek bait for the next 3 nights and nailed a 400-pound bruin, whereas "Jimmy" went home with all his arrows intact, complaining, of course, that the outfitter and his guides were all crooks. He did see a sow with two cubs, however.

Does this mean that all guides are experts? Of course not. Sometimes they do not understand the special needs of a bowhunter or muzzleloader hunter. Your job then is to educate them to the limitations of the sport. Remember, guided hunts are really team sports, and the better you and your guide work together, the more likely you will be going home with a trophy.

2. WRONG EQUIPMENT FOR THE JOB

Most outfitters have compiled an equipment list worked out after years of experience. It is to their advantage that you arrive in camp with suitable clothing and the proper tackle. This helps the camp run smoothly and increases your odds of having a successful trip.

The list does not mean, however, that you can make substitutions without first getting an okay from the outfitter. One western outfitter, for instance, asked his clients to bring riding boots with narrow toes, not felt-lined packs.

Running your own bait line is always a lot of work but very rewarding.

They would be spending a lot of time on horseback he told them and sliding a pair of thick-soled, rubber-bottomed packs into a pair of stirrups could make riding difficult. The outfitter also advised each hunter to bring a sling for his bow.

Well, you guessed it; one nimrod shows up in camp with two pairs of calf-high, heavy-duty, size 13 felt boots and no bow sling. He had all he could do to squeeze his boots into the stirrups, which was bad enough, but he had even more trouble extricating his boots from those stirrups when it was time to dismount. This can be a dangerous practice if the horse decides to run off with one of your feet still stuck in the stirrups. We used a length of cord and fashioned a bow sling for him, but he had to finish the late autumn hunt by riding bootless. Brrrr!

The moral of this story is simple. Don't question the outfitter's wisdom from your living room 3000 miles away! If the outfitter tells you to bring high-quality, heavy-duty rain gear, don't pack a flimsy disposable plastic suit just so you can save a few dollars. If he suggests a pair of full-size, eight-power binoculars, don't bring a pair of mini-6Xs.

Does this mean the outfitter is always right? Hardly! One year an outfitter talked me into getting into his Cessna 180 for a quick flight to a neighboring camp. We were bowhunting for caribou, but I also wanted to photograph some bears. We would be back before dark

he assured me, with plenty of photos. Well, it took a half dozen attempts to get airborne because the lake had whitecaps the size of four-man wall tents. The take-off scared the hell out of me (even he admitted to almost rolling the plane), and then to top things off, there were no caribou or bears at his other camp. This guy could talk the talk, but in no way could he walk the walk.

That pilot by the way killed himself and two hunters the following fall after crashing his plane on take-off. He thought he was a real bush pilot, but the whitecaps proved otherwise. Today, I won't get into a floatplane without a sleeping bag and a toothbrush. And I won't fly with a hot dog, either.

3. TOO TIRED TO FINISH

The first night of any camp is generally filled with high spirits and plenty of enthusiasm. Heck, we all like to make new friends and exchange hunting stories, but starting the hunt out on 2 hours of sleep the next morning can leave you overly tired for the rest of the trip. In fact, lack of proper rest is probably the number one reason why good hunters fail to fill a tag on an outfitted hunt. They are just too pooped to hunt effectively all week long.

A few years back, I was in a combo bear-elk camp with two guys that, with the help of a bottle of bourbon, burned their candles at both ends, keeping the camp half awake until the wee hours of the morning with their gibberish.

The best bear country can often be accessed by canoe.

Not surprisingly, they were both exhausted and all done hunting by the middle of the week and elected to sleep in when the cook woke us up for breakfast.

That didn't sit right with the outfitter, who based his reputation on the high success rates of his clients. "All right you two, get your butts out of bed right now," he yelled that frosty morning. "You are not staying in camp alone. The horses are saddled and ready to go. You either get up and ready to ride right now or get up and pack your bags. If you are not down by the corral in ten minutes, the cook will drive you back to town. And forget about getting a refund. I met my end of the bargain. You don't want to hunt, then you are going home!"

Those two bear hunters did get out of bed but were miserable the rest of the week. They blamed the outfitter's hard-driving attitude for their lack of success, but the truth of the matter is they failed because they wanted to party more than they wanted to hunt.

4. ATTITUDE UNBECOMING AN OFFICER

Big-game camps usually run smoothly, with clients remaining cordial for the duration of the trip. In fact, it is not all that unusual for hunters to make plans to share a camp again sometime in the future. But once in a great while, things fall apart. Anything can trigger a change in atmosphere, from a client feeling overwhelming pressure

to punch a tag to outright jealousy that a trophy animal was taken by someone else. Whatever the reason, the hunt of a lifetime can suddenly become the hunt from Hades.

The worst I ever witnessed took place in a wilderness black bear camp a decade ago. "Steve," who owned an archery pro shop, started criticizing the outfitter and his staff before he ever arrived in camp. By mid-week, "Steve" was throwing temper tantrums that included tossing food across the table and threatening to bring physical harm to the outfitter. His sarcastic and argumentative behavior seemed to mask a certain fear of failure, and no amount of reassurance could calm him. It wasn't until the rest of the hunters told him to clean up his act or he would be forced from camp did he begin to settle down. Even so, he did not fill a tag. My guess is that his sharp tongue with the guides, who undoubtedly repaid him in spades, and his lack of patience on stand cost him dearly.

Fortunately, these are rare events. Nonetheless, you can avoid hunters with big egos and those with chips on their shoulders by choosing your hunting partners carefully. A good booking agent can also help screen unsavory people from your camp thus increasing your odds of a positive experience.

5. LISTEN TO THE MAN!

One of the reasons we hire outfitters and guides is to lead us to an area teaming with wild game and then to help

Bait stations should be a mile or more apart from each other, and set up in areas known to harbor a good population of black bears.

Spring bear hunting and spring fishing go hand-in-hand. This stream was noted for its native brook trout. Other camps offer great northern pike and walleye fishing.

us pick out a trophy specimen. In the case of black bears, they can be quite difficult to field judge if you have never seen one in the wild before. In fact, at first glance ALL black bears look huge, even from a distance. It therefore behooves us to rely on a guide/outfitter's experience and trained eye to steer us in the right direction.

You don't want to shoot the first bear you see until you get a handle on field judging them yourself. Of course, not all clients take the advice of their guide or outfitter. Some seem to think they know better and actually do the opposite of what they are told to do.

A case in point took place several years ago when I was in a bear camp where the guide told an over-gunned client that two bears were visiting a particular bait site. The first one came in early and probably weighed 100 pounds. The second bruin, however, was a real keeper, a 400-pounder with jet-black fur. This big old boar only visited the bait site near dusk, and even then, he only showed up every other night.

"Don't shoot the first bear you see," was the guide's parting advice when we dropped the nimrod off that evening. "Remember, the big bear won't show until last shooting light."

Well, an hour before sunset a bear appeared at the bait site, and the client nailed it with his 458. The bear only traveled a few yards after the shot, nearly cut in two by the heavy-grained bullet. The client, not knowing for sure if his bear was indeed dead, elected to wait on stand. As darkness came, our hero heard a twig snap behind the bait, and, you guessed it, a boar four times the weight of the earlier bear appeared next to the bait barrel.

The guide just shook his head when he heard the story and refrained from saying, "I told you so." But in the end, the client went home happy. He had his bear, and I'm sure the story he told his friends about how he shot in self-defense made him look good in front of his buds.

And what happened to that big boar? It doesn't take a bear very long to smarten up and become unkillable. In fact, that giant bruin made it through the rest of the bear season, as evidenced by his wide tracks around the bait barrel, but he was never seen again.

But that's what usually happens to trophy animals when you try to guide the guide, bring the wrong equipment, are too tired to hunt hard all week, come to camp packing an attitude or simply fail to heed the advice you contracted for: They walk out of your life forever. And you know what? In these cases, it is nobody's fault but your own!

Some outfitters cater to bowhunters; others don't have a clue.

Assuming the outfitter does his job, whose fault is it when we return to camp empty-handed?

If you have never hunted bears before, listen carefully to your guide's advice. After all, that's what you paid him for.

Retrieving horses is just one of the many chores guides are expected to do, even when you fail to bring the required riding boots.

Reading Big Bear Sign

If you want to shoot a really big bear, you better learn sign language!

If you like to bow hunt big bears, this bait site was a dream come true. The bait barrel was secured at the bottom of a small rise a few yards from the shoreline of a large wilderness lake, and it was kept filled to the brim with donuts and sweet honey. There were several trails leading in and out of the site, and all were littered with plenty of fresh tracks on top of plenty of old tracks. I was certain that up to two dozen bruins were exiting the nearby thick bush to feed here on a regular basis.

Most all the tracks were average in size, which told me that the vast majority of bruins were sows and yearlings. It was also just as obvious that a large boar had visited the bait site at least once over the past week or so, as evidenced by the seven-inch-plus claw marks he left on the fir tree next to the bait barrel.

This boar was definitely worth waiting for, and if I was careful, I thought I might find out just how big this fella really was. I didn't know it then, but I would have to wait two full weeks before I would have that boar within range of my bow.

Indeed, "Ironsides" came in unannounced, on the heels of an estrous sow, on the last evening of my hunt. It was plain to see she had been at the bait site before, for after testing the wind, she sauntered right up to the barrel and began chowing down. The 675-pound boar with a head the size of a peach basket was much more cautious, however. It took him 20 minutes to work himself in close to the barrel, and even then, he did so by stopping often near every rock, stump and log. It was a magnificent sight watching that bear work the cover, one of nature's true stalkers in action.

Eventually, he made it to the barrel, and although he grabbed a few donuts, Ironsides never let the sow get too far away from him. And because my back was to the lake, he also never gave me a killing shot angle. Instinctively perhaps, he kept his back towards the bush while facing the

unfamiliar territory around the bait site head on. The best angle I had was a sharp quartering to, which is really no shot at all. When the sow exited the bait site, the cautious boar left too, padding out of my life forever.

BIG BEAR SIGN

How did we know there was a book bear at that particular bait? We read the sign! In the past, many outfitters just plopped their clients into a stand with little or no say-so, but today you can just as easily book with an outfitter who will run a bait line for you, and then let you choose your own stand(s) when you come into camp. Either way, you can increase your chances of bagging a trophy bruin if you learn to ask the outfitter the right questions, or if you can properly interpret the bear sign around the bait yourself.

How then can you tell which bait has the best bruin? For starters, big boars don't advertise their presence in a manner that smaller bears, yearlings, and sows with cubs so often do. So, you'll want to examine each bait site carefully and weigh all the "soft" evidence before you elect to sit over one particular bait. This goes whether you book an all-inclusive hunt with an outfitter, "rent" a dozen baits from a local guide, or plan a do-it-yourself trip with a buddy.

When you examine a bait site, start by looking for bear tracks in the nearby mud, sand or soft earth. They are hard to find, but a front pad better than 5 inches in width is usually a very good bear (the rear pad resembles a barefoot person). Creek beds, logging roads, gravel bars and beaver dams are all good places to look for tracks. Keep in mind that large bears rarely approach a bait station on a daily basis, while subordinate bears will feed almost daily. Indeed, those "old" tracks you found on the beaver dam might in fact be heralding a return visit by that bruin in a day or two.

You should have no trouble locating entrance and

How do you know when a boar this size is hanging around? You read the sign!

Front and rear pads are uniquely different. This is a front pad print.

exit trails if the bait is being hit regularly. If so, examine nearby trees for more bear sign. Claw marks up the trunk will give you clues as to how tall the bear is, and the space between individual clawings can give you a sense of how wide his front pads might be. Fresh beds on the trail or near the bait site can also indicate relative body size. Be aware that bears will often sit on their haunches, like a dog, leaving smaller "beds" than if they were lying on their belly. Finally, if the nearby brush is thick, look for bear "tunnels" hollowed out of the branches and leaves and for bear fur stuck to those branches. This is an excellent way to determine the color(s) of the bear(s) feeding there.

Of course, seeing a big bear within a half-mile of any bait station is a good sign, even if that particular bait has not yet been hit. Sooner or later, that bear will sniff out your pile of goodies and sneak in to check it out. When he does, he may not leave any obvious clues behind, such as tracks or claw marks, and he may or may not sample the food.

He will often, however, first circle the bait, staying under cover and just within sight of your offering. You will have to look closely, maybe even get on your hands and knees, as the trail will be faint. Look for wide pad impressions in the dead leaves, crushed vegetation and bear hair stuck in the bark of nearby tree trunks. You may also find logs ripped apart, overturned stones and ankle-high vegetation ripped out of the ground all along this trail, indi-

cating the bear was feeding as he was watching. You may even find where he laid down on his belly facing the bait as if he was carefully studying the set-up (he was!).

This trail is undoubtedly one of the surest signs you have a big bear working the area and one of the most overlooked pieces of big-bear evidence available. Locating it usually separates the casual bear hunter from the real expert.

Another clue you have a dominate bear sniffing around is when you stumble upon several large piles of fresh dung 1.5 to 2 inches in diameter scattered around the bait site. I've found THE stand to hunt when scat such as this seems to be placed purposely on entrance and exit trails. Any droppings the size of a soft drink can indicate a very big boar has taken over the bait site, claiming it as his own with his specially scented territorial marker. My impression is that these strategically deposited droppings also function as a warning sign to other male bears telling them to keep out, and if any other boar dares to trespass, he does so at great risk. We will talk about this more later.

All else being equal, the absence of small-bear sign is sometimes a good indication a decent bear is in the area. If you must flip a coin, lean towards bait sites located in clearings adjacent to thick underbrush because these locations provide cover that draws larger bears. Keep in mind that your best chance at a bear will be on the first

Bear tracks are a dead giveaway as to the size of the bear. Except in the extreme northern portions of their range, any front pad 5 inches wide or better has an 18-inch or better skull.

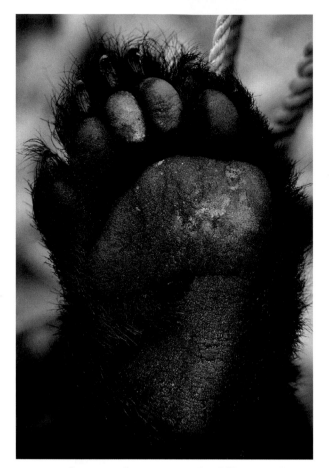

Front and rear pads are uniquely different. The rear resembles a barefoot person.

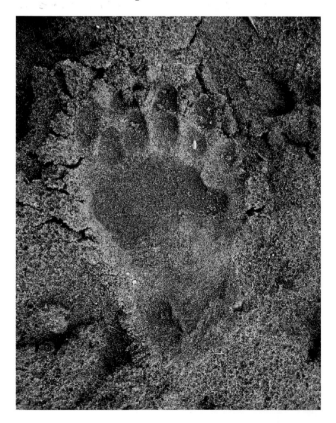

There is no doubt that field-judging black bears is a tough assignment in the wild. At first glance, all bears look big, but there are some body parts you can zero in on to help you eliminate the subordinate specimens from the real jumbos.

First, you must determine the sex of the bruin, as most trophy black bears are boars. Males have a penile sheath, much like that of a dog, so look for a few curly hairs on his belly near his rear legs. Boars also fight often, so any bear that has facial scars and torn ears is one to take a second look at.

Many hunters will tell you that a big boar has a head shaped like a pumpkin, complete with small ears, but you have to see a lot of bears to be able to pick up on this. I find it better to look at his shoulders, belly, and then his hams. A big boar has massive shoulders, much like that of a pro linebacker, which is one reason their heads look small in comparison to the rest of their body. In addition, a big boar most always drags his belly at or near the ground, whereas smaller bears do not. Belly draggers are most definitely shooters. A big boar also has a big wide butt, unlike sows and young boars, who have rather unremarkable hind ends. Keep in mind that if you have to somehow justify the body parts as belonging to a trophy bruin, then that bear is probably not a real shooter.

Finally, there is the demeanor. A mature boar, although sneaky, also knows he is the king of the forest, and he acts accordingly. If your instincts tell you that a particular bear is nothing to fool with, then you are probably looking at one heck of a bear. Shoot him, you won't be sorry!

Use your head when hunting bomber bears. They are very intelligent animals!

night you hunt from the stand. Once the bear knows you're sneaking around the bait, he'll be much more difficult to bag.

Take Ironsides for example. There was no other big-bear sign near the bait site nor had there been any sightings of him in the general vicinity. If I had not glanced up

A bear will often sit on his haunches, like a dog, leaving a smaller circle of crushed vegetation than if he was lying on his belly.

the trunk of the tree looking for claw marks, it would have been easy to dismiss this bait site as holding only sows. But boars go on the prowl for estrous sows in late spring and early summer. Thus, any bait site with this many potential mates running around at this time of the year is a site to be coveted.

BLACK BEAR BEHAVIOR

Behavior of other bears at the site can be another indication a dominant bruin is working a particular bait. For example, a yearling bruin may eat nervously or very early in the evening, and then bolt at the slightest noise. I once watched a yearling bear announce his arrival at a bait site by snapping branches and then huffing, puffing and popping his jaws. "A little like a teenager whistling in the dark," I thought to myself later. I guess he didn't want to run into any "big" surprises at the dinner table!

Indeed, one of the biggest mistakes neophytes make is shooting the first bear that comes to the bait. There is a social hierarchy among bears and in no place is this more evident than around a bait site. Sows, yearlings and young boars often feed first in the early evening followed by bears higher up the social ladder, the biggest boars feeding last when they feel it is safest.

A subordinate boar will generally announce his arrival by purposely snapping a twig, which warns any

bears already on the bait that he is nearby. Bears subordinate to him will generally melt back into the forest in anticipation of his arrival. The snapping of a twig also serves as a safety device for the arriving bear as well. The last thing he wants to do is surprise the alpha male at the feeding site. He knows from past experience that he is no match for the dominant bruin.

BLACK BEAR SCHOOL

Checking bait sites is much like running a trap line. Nearby sign can give you plenty of clues as to the size, sex, and color of the bear as well as its feeding habits, breeding status and general behavior traits. Taken together, they should help you choose one bait station or hunting area over another. Study these next scenarios before your next trip afield, and I think you will see what I mean. Again, keep in mind that almost all book black bears are boars.

END-OF-THE-ROAD BAIT

The first bait your guide shows you has been placed inside an abandoned logging chute at the end of a 4x4 trail. Visibility is good up and down the old road, giving you plenty of shooting light even under low-light conditions. If there is a big bear on this bait, you will have plenty of time to size him up before you take your shot, even if he comes in late. And speaking of taking a shot, there are also plenty of trees along the edge of the road,

Droppings strategically placed around a food source seem to serve both as a territorial marker and as a warning sign to other boars to keep out. Large, mature boars have droppings the diameter of soft drink cans.

which make it an ideal location for a rifle hunter, a muzzle-loader or even a bowhunter.

The guide tells you the bait has been hammered almost every night for nearly two weeks. He guarantees you that you will see a bear the first time you climb into your stand if you are patient and remain still. You look around as the bait barrel is being replenished and notice there are several trails leading in and out of the area, and bits of food are scattered all over the site. In fact, there is so much of a mess, it looks like a tornado touched down nearby.

CLEAR-CUT BAIT

The second treestand is in the middle of a two-year-old clear-cut. There's not much ground cover near the bait, but there are 5-inch pad marks along one of the nearby logging roads. It is undoubtedly a book animal, and your hopes soar.

A seasoned bear hunter sat over the bait for several evenings, but the bear would not approach the bait during legal shooting hours, preferring instead to weave in and out of the brush growing along the far edge of the cut. Although the hunter was able to sneak out of his treestand each evening without spooking the bear, the outfitter blames that hunter for not getting a shot because he was too fidgety in the stand.

SWAMP BAIT

The third bait is situated at the foot of a narrow ridge that rises out of a large, impenetrable swamp. It is an ideal bedding area for bears, and the mile-long ridge is a natural travel corridor that connects the swamp with several adjacent beech ridges. The spruce and fir trees are so thick here daylight barely reaches the forest floor, making it a scary place to be even in the middle of the day. The trail to the bow stand, however, is well marked.

The outfitter advises you to stay aloft until the very last second of legal shooting light. Getting in and out of the Swamp Bait gives him the jitters, however, so he hands you a lever-action 30-30 "just in case" you run into a bear on the trail. Then he advises you to wear a head net, plenty of insect repellent and to carry a spare flashlight. The bait is only being hit once or twice a week, but almost all the bait is taken on each visit. There are no well-defined trails leading to or from the bait.

REPORT CARD

Which of these three stands would you choose, and how would you hunt it? Well, the "End of the Road" sounds like the ideal black bear set-up, but only if you have never seen a bear before or if all you want to do is take pictures. It is probably being hit every evening by a sow with a couple of cubs. The cubs knock the grass

Locating the trail a boar uses to survey a bait site often separates the casual bear hunter from the real expert.

Sows with cubs, yearlings and small boars leave plenty of sign around a bait site. The absence of such sign often indicates a larger bear is in the neighborhood.

down and scatter food all around like a pack of first graders. To confirm your suspicions, simply check the immediate vicinity for small tracks and droppings in the half-inch diameter range. Food containers punctured with narrow tooth impressions will also indicate the presence of this year's cubs.

The second bear at the Clear-Cut Bait is bait-shy due to the lack of adequate cover near the bait, which causes the bear to wait until after dark to visit. This is the outfitter's fault. He should have put the bait in a more strategic location just off the clear-cut—maybe at the top of a ravine for example—to take full advantage of both available ground cover and local topography. If a bear doesn't feel safe at the bait, he won't expose himself and come in to chow down until darkness overtakes the landscape. An experienced outfitter would know that.

Stand three at the Swamp Bait is the best of the lot. Any place that scares you has massive bruin written all over it. Big old boars are extremely solitary, except during the mating season, and there's no better place to be left alone than an impenetrable tangle out in the middle of nowhere. In addition, that ridge is a natural highway in and out of the swamp, which doubles your chances of a sighting. I would hunt this stand in the absence of big bear sign simply because of the topography! Indeed, I have arrowed three book bears from such places, and now my friends and I race to these sights even if fresh sign is scant.

Timing is the key, however. Don't sit in the stand until you fully expect the bear to show. If he is hitting the bait every second or third night, hunt elsewhere for a night or two. Your best chance of tagging this bear is on the first night you hunt it, so wait for all the conditions to be in your favor before you climb aloft.

PINE TREE BAIT

Here are three more choices. The Pine Tree Bait is being hit on a regular basis, almost every night according to the outfitter, by an average bear. You know he is not the king of the woods, but you know you can't tag a record-book bear on every trip either. You decide to sit over the bait, and an hour before dark, a 200-pound boar sneaks in for a bite to eat. Just before he reaches the barrel, however, he hunches his back up, turns away from the bait and hisses before disappearing back into the bush. The rest of the evening is uneventful, but the next morning the guide tells you the bait was cleaned out.

PIE-PLATE BEAR

Your guide shows you one of the camp's newest baits. When you get to the bait barrel, he shows you a well-concealed stand and two trails leading in and out of the thick brush adjacent to the bait barrel. As you step closer, you find you can easily pick out pie-plate-size impressions on those trails leading to and from the barrel. They look big,

Subordinate bears will often announce their arrival to a bait station by purposely snapping a twig. Once alerted, smaller bears will melt back into the bush. This is also a safety valve for the incoming bear. He knows what will happen if he surprises a bigger and more powerful bear at the feeding site. He'll get his butt kicked!

but they are difficult to size accurately because they are blurred beyond their normal size. Obviously, the bear has been placing his feet in the exact same tracks each time he visits, which has been about every other night for the past 8 to 10 days. Nobody has sat over this bait yet.

LOVE BAIT

It is late spring, and you have yet to see a shooter bear. The outfitter takes you to another bait site that is being hit seemingly all day long by as many as 20 bears. Unfortunately, judging from the size of the tracks, none of the bears weigh more than 150 pounds. There is, however, a set of large bear tracks on the edge of a nearby river. The tracks are a week or so old but are deep and wide, indicating a shooter was in the vicinity.

REPORT CARD

What choices! Each bait holds a shooter bear! Let's start with the Pine Tree Bait. It has at least two bears in attendance, one of which is a dominant male. Most hunters, given the opportunity, would have shot the small boar, but if you are looking for a mature bear, that would be a mistake. The body language of the small boar alone should have been enough to tell you a bigger bear was in the vicinity. Indeed, small bears are scared to death of mature boars!

The Pine Tree Bear is very cautious approaching

the bait. He is actually sneaking in by taking it one step at a time. I say "he" because sows and immature boars often rush into a feeding area with wild abandon. A mature boar, on the other hand, will undoubtedly take his sweet time and come in very carefully, stepping in the same places each time he visits. This is one way big bears make themselves vulnerable. A portable treestand set up on the off side of a large tree could be your ticket to success here, if you can wait for a quartering away angle.

The last stand, the Love Bait, is undoubtedly a magnet for sows, and as breeding season nears, it will also attract mature boars. Even though those big tracks along the river are old and faded, take heart. The boar was keeping tabs on that bait site, and when the breeding urges take hold, he will be back for a second look-see. He could show up almost any night, so stick with it.

TROPHY BAIT

Let's keep going with three more bait scenarios. This first treestand is a chip shot away from a cribbed bait hidden along the edge of a large swamp. There are two trails the bears seem to be using to enter and exit the baited area. It is one of the outfitter's favorite sites because his clients have tagged several book bears here. He tells you the bait is being hit sporadically by a bear with 6.5-inch front pads. Lately it seems whenever a bowhunter sits near the bait, however, all he sees is mosquitoes. A few of

A sow and cubs will devastate a bait station.

those hunters report hearing twigs snap downwind of the stand right around prime time. Two or three nights after the bowhunter abandons the site, the bear returns and hits the bait again, leaving impressions of his big pads all around the bait site.

CLOCKWORK ORANGE

The second treestand is adjacent to a new bait located in a wooded hollow. The ground around the bait is wet and spongy with a bumper crop of new spring greenery. The outfitter tells you the bait is being hit every second night like clockwork by a bear with a 5-inch front pad. This bear takes the same trail to the bait by placing his feet in the exact same tracks each time he visits. He then circles the barrel, squeezes through a tight thicket, steps just over an 8-inch log and approaches the mouth of the barrel using the surrounding brush to his advantage.

PASTURE BAIT

The third treestand is located in a grown-over pasture 100 yards from an oat field. The outfitter has baited the area with oats, honey and plenty of meat by-products. The farmer tells you there are plenty of bears around as they are gorging themselves on his crops. As you approach the field for the first time, you see a very large bruin feeding in the oats not far from the bait. You watch him as he eventually takes the path that leads to the bait and your treestand.

REPORT CARD

Where should you hunt? Obviously, there is a book bear on the first set-up, the Trophy Bait, that is well worth any effort you might extend. The bear is bait-wise, but is attracted to the goodies nonetheless. Over the years, he has probably been here many times. What the bear is doing is circling downwind of the treestand before committing himself to the bait. If he smells a stinky human, as he has apparently done in the past, he simply wanders elsewhere. If the coast is clear, he approaches the bait along one of the well-worn trails.

The snapping of twigs should give you a clue as to the bear's patrol route. Check it out early the next morning by looking for bent vegetation and fresh depressions in the soft turf. One trick is to set up an ambush downwind of this route, and then wait a few days for the bear to start hitting the bait again. Don't wait too long, however. As soon as this bear finds another food source, he'll likely abandon the site altogether.

The bruin working Clockwork Orange is in all likelihood a big bear, although the spongy and damp earth my lead you to believe the track is bigger than it really is. He is, however, very cagey and very cautious. And I say "he" because the odds are this bear is an old boar. Why? A sow generally steps over a log with little concern, but a boar is much more cautious, preferring to place his

Open clear-cuts provide little cover for black bears and are thus poor locations for bait stations.

Timing is one of the keys to success. Don't climb aloft until you are sure all the conditions are perfect. Once a big bear knows you are after him, you probably won't ever see him again.

This bear has you spotted. Notice the tree step. Why aren't you in your stand?

front pad only an inch or so past the edge of the log when he crosses.

How big is he? Look for a "bear bed" at first light. A bruin will often lie down near the bait to feed. Look for bent and broken spring growth for a better idea as to his body size. What color is this bear? That's easy, too. Stick your hand inside that thicket and pull out a few body hairs that invariably get stuck there. Another good place to look for bear hair is at the base of nearby trees.

You have an excellent chance of bagging this bruin your first night on stand if the wind stays in your favor. Remember, he's not expecting any trouble so wait for the bear to get to the barrel and turn broadside or quartering away before you shoot.

The Pasture Bait is a no brainer. The outfitter has done his job and now it is up to you to wait for the perfect shot. Wear rubber boots to your stand and do not walk on the same trail as the bear. It may take several days for a big bear to return, but he will as long as there's plenty of food nearby. I took a 450 to 500-pound book boar one autumn on just such a set-up.

PLENTY BEARS

All right, it's the end of the spring season, and you still haven't gotten a shot at a bear. It's also your last night in camp. The outfitter knows you are running out of time, and gives you three more choices. He has one stand that's being hit nightly, but by half a dozen sows and yearlings. There isn't a big bear in the lot, but a gargantuan boar was seen there last year just about this time.

CREEK BAIT

His second bait has not yet been hit even though it is situated near the confluence of a creek and a small river. However, a very big bear was seen near the site last week when the outfitter checked the bait. The brush covering the barrel appeared to have been disturbed, but no bait was taken. Other than that, the set-up has been a let down for the outfitter.

BONUS BAIT

This bait is only a short distance from camp and has a permanent tower built in plain sight 20 yards from the bait. The open areas behind the bait station are littered with bear trails and plenty of tracks, including one main trail that comes out of the deep bush and crosses a beaver dam within sight of the bait 100 yards distant.

Your guide tells you that there is at least one huge bear working this bait station, and when you see all the 5-inch front pad tracks, you believe him. It seems like such a sure thing you are ready to climb into the stand right then and there to begin the hunt.

Big bears like to circle downwind before committing themselves to your set-up.

The sign was sparse, but we all agreed a good bear was working the bait. The author took this bear while hunting in Alberta with Bob Heyde and his uncle, Jake Newfeld, of Homestead Outfitters.

REPORT CARD

On the surface, the Bonus Bait seems to be the most promising of the three, but it is not. Like the Clear-Cut Bait, this stand is too open for a big bear to approach in broad daylight. Oh, he's there all right, but he isn't hitting the bait until well after dark. A battery-operated timer can verify this for you in short order. The problem is that everyone in camp has probably sat over this bait at one time or another, effectively educating the bear. This is a stand for the camp know-it-all or the camp smart-mouth. He thinks he is getting a good deal when in fact he has been effectively dealt out of the game altogether. There is a way to tag this bear, however, which we will discuss when we talk strategies for finicky bruins.

What about the other two choices? If this were an early spring hunt, I would choose the Creek Bait over Plenty Bears. Big boars often scout out a bait site carefully before committing themselves. It is not uncommon for an early spring bear to sniff around a bait barrel for up to a week or so before tearing into the bait. Part of the reason for this is their weak digestive system. They have not yet got the juices flowing, so to speak, and are unable to take advantage of much other than spring greenery. The fact a good bear was seen in the vicinity is enough to hold my interest.

HOW MUCH DID HE WEIGH?

The live weight of a black bear is difficult to field judge in the woods. Their roly-poly appearance, long hairs and the fact few of us see many bears "on the pad" or even at weigh-in stations simply compounds the problem. Use the following chart to estimate the live weight of your bear:

Girth (inches)	Live Weight (pounds)
25	65
26	73
27	81
28	89
29	98
30	108
31	117
32	128
33	138
34	149
35	161
36	173
37	185
38	198
39	211
40	225
41	239
42	253
43	268
44	284
45	300
46	316
47	332
48	350
49	367
50	385
51	403
52	422
53	442
54	461
55	481
56	502
57	522
58	544
59	566
60	588

Learning to field-judge black bears is critical when trying to tag a trophy bruin.

If you are looking for a 400-pounder, it is to your advantage to check as many baits as possible.

- Looking for bear sign around a bait site is often the key to success. It is, therefore, to your advantage to see firsthand as many bait sites as possible when hunting with an outfitter. This practice should be agreed upon BEFORE you book the hunt!

- Your best chances of taking any particular bear is to wait for him to get accustomed to the site, then sneak in when the conditions are perfect. Once a mature boar knows you are after him, he will likely abandon the site altogether. Use your head; you are hunting a very intelligent animal!

- Besides size, color can also denote trophy quality. Black bears can have red, cinnamon, blond and chocolate hides as well as the very rare white. Look for hair caught on nearby tree trunks, brush or even a length of barbed wire left purposely near the bait for clues to coat color (HINT!). There is no finer trophy in the world than an off-color record-book bruin!

- Unless hunting in the extreme north, like the Yukon or Northwest Territories, any front pad that measures 5 or more inches in width is probably a book bear for archers and muzzleloaders.

- Can't find a bear track near a bait site? Spread cooking oil, grease or even just water near the bait site to help soften the soil. The oil/grease will also go a long ways towards attracting still more bears. Put some grease on the trunks of nearby trees, too, to help lure bears to the bait site, and then gauge any fresh claw marks found on the tree's trunk for body size.

- If you know a trophy bear has visited the site early in the season, stick with it. Sooner or later, he will reappear. I once sat over a bait for almost two weeks waiting for a gargantuan bear to return. I'd like to tell you I shot him, but (gulp!) I missed an easy 15-yard shot with my bow!

- Mature boars have larger territories than sows, one reason a big boar will hit a bait site only every second or third day.

- Scout entrance and exit trails carefully. You may find an alternate treestand site should you need one later. You might also get an idea where the bear is bedding, in case you need to move the bait barrel.

- There is a hierarchy among bears, and a mature boar will often take over the best cover. Any place that gives you the willies is a prime big bear hideout. I have taken three Pope & Young boars in just such places, and now my friends and I fight for this type of stand even if fresh bear sign is scant.

- Like depositing dung on entrance and exit trails, clawing tree trunks and biting branches and forest service road signs, the snapping of twigs around a bait site or any area bears are known to congregate is a form of bear communication that needs further study. One of their functions seems to be Mother Nature's way of avoiding deadly conflict. These various forms of black bear sign language may also serve as advertisements for the breeding season, much like scrapes do for whitetail deer.

Bears communicate with each other in ways we are only now just beginning to understand.

However, since it is nearly mating season, I would choose Plenty Bears over all three simply because of the number of sows and the fact that a big bear was seen there last year. Boars travel widely looking for sows in early summer, and there is no better bait than a half-dozen female beauties gathered in one location. And as a plus, we know that big bears have excellent memories, especially for food sources, and tend to return year after year to check it out. Thus, the likelihood of last year's trophy returning this spring is not out of the question.

Keep in mind, however, that if a mature boar visits a bait site to hook up with a sow or comes into a bait following a sow near estrous, you will probably have only one opportunity at him. So don't wait for the perfect shot; take the first good opportunity that presents itself, because when they exit a bait site at this time of the season, they are unlikely to return. It seems they go to parts unknown to breed without interference from other boars.

As you can see, black bears are not the dumb, roly-poly creatures they are so often made out to be. If you want to get a crack at an honest-to-goodness trophy bruin, be it over bait in the spring or by sneaking and peeking along a berry patch in the fall, you have to first locate and then interpret black bear sign accurately. After all, they leave plenty of it around.

The Art and Science of Baiting Bears

Here are some tips and tactics for your next setup!

The site intrigued me. It was situated at the confluence of two streams, a natural crossing for black bears, and well off the beaten path. It was also dark under the canopy of spruce and fir, even on a bright sunlit day, which gave me the willies whenever I replenished the bait. Indeed, the 5-inch front pad tracks in the nearby mud indicated a mature boar was raiding my cache of meat and pastries every other night or so, and the last thing I wanted to do was come face to face with him in the poor light.

After one of his visits, I hung a portable stand crosswind to the pile of logs covering the bait, and even though I was anxious to loose an arrow, I waited for the bear to get used to the new set-up before climbing onboard. It was the right decision, for the first night I hid aloft, the big bear circled cautiously downwind of the bait site, and once satisfied all was safe, committed himself to the offering just before dark.

I waited for him to present a quartering-away shot, and when he did, I came to full draw, aimed and released a vaned shaft at his vitals in one fluid motion. The Pope & Young bruin let out a deafening roar upon impact and immediately fled the scene with his stubby tail tucked between his legs like a scalded dog. His efforts were to no avail, however, as he was already dead on his feet, expiring less than 50 yards from my stand.

LOCATING HOT BAIT SITES

Baiting is by far the most popular hunting method for black bears in Canada. Except for British Columbia, baiting is encouraged in every province that borders the United States, plus Nova Scotia, Newfoundland and Labrador. It is also presently legal in nine states and accounts for more entries in the various record books than stalking, tracking, still-hunting, calling and running them with dogs combined.

But setting up a proper ambush is not so easy a task. For openers, black bears are secretive creatures of the deep woods and dark swamps. Even in farm country, they seem to thrive on the edge, padding carefully about those nasty, hard-to-reach tangles of brush, boulders and fallen snags. Oh, you will see them feeding in the wee hours along the edges of clear-cuts, open meadows and wind-swept ridges, but their daytime lair will most always be in the thickest and most impenetrable cover available. Even when on the prowl for food or mates, black bears, and especially big boars, choose routes that offer them the most protection.

Even so, it has been said that enticing a bear to a bait site is not a difficult task. Indeed, try hiding a cooler of meat or a couple bags of groceries in bear country, and see what happens! It shouldn't take more than a couple days or so for a bear to find your goodies and devour them without so much as a "by your leave."

What is difficult, however, is meeting that bear at your bait site during legal shooting hours. Big boars are smart, very smart, and that means you have to plan your ambush well ahead of time. A bag of pastries tossed on the shoreline may attract a roaming bear, but there is no guarantee that he will give you a clear shot unless you pay close attention to all the details.

So where do you start? When it comes to choosing a spot for a bait site, your number one concern should be: Location! Location! Location! And that means setting up near a bear's primary bedding zone, his preferred feeding area or along a likely travel route. You do not want to waste your time trying to lure a trophy boar into an ambush site that suits just you because he will undoubtedly be a no-show.

Instead, to maximize your chances of attracting a mature boar in close enough for a good shot, you must first pick a spot a bear would likely visit during daylight hours. Then you have to figure out a way to be there

Mature bruins prefer plenty of cover around a bait station. Even though I was careful, this bear heard my approach.

The number one rule to successful bear baiting: Location, Location, Location!

when he arrives without spooking him into the next state or province.

TREESTAND RULES

For best results, locate a suitable tree for your treestand BEFORE beginning your baiting operation. On more than one occasion I have visited a hot bait site teeming with big bear sign only to realize there was not a suitable tree nearby in which to erect a stand. Even if you choose to hunt at ground zero, you must pick a shooting location first before you start your baiting operation.

Because your chances are best from an elevated platform, your goal should be to erect a stand 12 to 15 feet off the ground and, if you are bowhunting or hunting with a pistol, no more than 20 yards from the bait. Riflemen and muzzleloader users can back off accordingly, but then you miss out on all the excitement of being within spitting distance of a wild bruin!

You also want to approach your stand quietly, without going near the bait. If a big bear knows you've been at the bait recently, he may very well retreat until after dark. Keep in mind that once a bear claims a food source as his own, he often camps out nearby. Thus, any noise out of the ordinary, such as the clack of metal or the squeak of a treestand, will raise his suspicions.

Here are some more tips to consider:
- Pick a large tree with many branches to help camou-

flage your silhouette, and arrange it so you can shoot your bow or rifle from a sitting position. Your goal is to sit dead still as the bruin approaches, and then remain that way until you are ready to shoot.
- Deep-woods bears have only moderate eyesight (by contrast, black bears that thrive in wide-open spaces have excellent eyesight!). They are not blind, however, and they do respond to movement very quickly. Full camouflage, including face, neck and hands will help you blend into your surroundings as well as disguise any involuntary movements.
- Conceal the entrance trail to your bait site as best you can, and if need be, park your 4x4 some distance away while replenishing baits. Anti-hunters, sightseers, other hunters and, yes, even other outfitters have been known to sabotage a legal set-up. A sign that says "Caution: Large Bear Traps in Use" tacked to a nearby tree might help keep the riffraff at bay.
- Force the bear into a broadside or quartering-away angle by cribbing the bait with logs, stones, etc. Any other shot angle is dangerous and unacceptable.
- There are two schools of thought concerning scent control. The first one says keep yourself and the site as free of human scent as possible. Rubber boots, charcoal-activated suits and scent eliminators help. The second says that since the bears

Erect your treestand with care. Be sure your entry and exit routes do not overlap those of the bear.

Take your time and crib your bait properly by making it tough to enter the bait by any other direction. A sly bear will try and sneak in the back door if you give him an opening. Look at all those mosquitoes!

already associate the food with human beings, do not make any effort to hide your odor. You can even leave articles of clothing behind to further desensitize the bear. Each school of thought has its merits.

In case you are wondering just how good a bear's nose is, take note of this. One evening I sat on a bait site for the first time that season. No one had been there before me, except of course to maintain the bait. I was conscious of my scent trail and took all the precautions I could think

of to be scent-free. That evening a 200-pound boar approached the bait station very slowly and very deliberately. It was probably the first time the bruin had visited the site, and he was making doubly sure he was safe by repeatedly testing the wind and sniffing every plant, tree trunk and log on his way to the bait barrel.

When he came upon my entrance path, he about flipped. As I recall, it took him about 10 minutes to eventually determine my direction of travel. He did this by carefully sniffing plant stems, blades of grass and new spring leaves. He could tell which way I headed by "simply" determining which side of the plant stem, blade of grass, or leaf carried my scent. Incredible!

He then backtracked my trail for 10 or 15 yards and stood motionless for several minutes staring back in the direction of my parked 4x4, about a mile away. Then he turned around and followed my scent right to the tree in which I was perched. Without hesitation he looked upwards, "woofed" once and stood up leaning his massive fore legs against the tree trunk. He knew exactly where I was! I remained as motionless as I could without coming unglued. The bear soon circled around

That incredible sniffer at work!

In the spring, black bears are attracted to water and all that spring greenery. Look for tracks and scat along shorelines and the juncture of feeder creeks.

behind me and without fanfare left the site, blending into the dark understory like a phantom. I never did see that bear again.

A dilemma often presents itself when it comes time to exit the stand. On the one hand, you can tiptoe out of there hoping that if there is a bear nearby, he won't hear you and thus ruin the surprise you have in store for him. Or, you can make a fair amount of noise, as if you are replenishing the bait barrel, and then be on your merry way. Your goal is to exit the scene without tipping the bear off to your intentions. However, you don't want to be so quiet that you inadvertently come face to face on the exit trail!

HOT SPRING BAIT SITES

When bears emerge from their dens in the spring, it takes their digestive tracts some time to adjust to the long period of hibernation. Red meat, carrion and even fish are often just too much for their system to handle. Spring greenery in the form of new shoots, green grasses, clover and the buds, leaves and catkins of the aspen tree are a few of the important foods bears seek out at this time. Here are some tips for hot spring bait sites:

- Water and sunshine promote the season's first greenery. Look for tracks and scat along the edges of rivers, lakes and other large bodies of water.
- Stream banks—especially where thick brush and uneven terrain make it difficult for humans to

walk—are natural travel lanes for mature boars.
- Bears always check out the confluence of two streams, where a river and a stream meet or where moving water enters and exits a lake or pond.
- Bears routinely patrol the edges of swamps. Expect increased activity along any ridge or finger of land that leads into or out of the swamp.
- Look for claw marks on the trunks of aspens and "bear nests" in the upper most branches, which indicate early spring feeding.
- In an effort to help hold the soil near construction projects, managers often plant clover. Look for this highly preferred delicacy near the edges of forest service roads, logging roads in and around re-claimed clear-cuts and maintenance roads along gas lines and wellheads. Power lines, gas lines, underground communications lines and other rights-of-ways are another area worth a careful look-see in early spring.
- Keep your bait stations at least a mile apart as the crow flies. It is not uncommon for a single bear to hit several bait sites in one evening if they are positioned in the same general vicinity of each other.
- If you are not sure when the bear is hitting your bait, affix a timer to one of the entrance or exit trails. You may learn that the bear is chowing down right after you leave for the evening or that he is

Ray Broughton uses a timer to learn if a bear has turned nocturnal.

"Stink" baits attract bears from miles around.

Staging areas allow you to check a bait site without disturbing the area.

more nocturnal than you thought, feeding after midnight. On rare occasions, a big bear may also feed at first light.

- Many outfitters, guides and do-it-yourself hunters use "stink baits" as a primary attractor, hoping the outlandish odors will quickly attract bears to the bait station. Where legal, rotting fish or beaver carcasses work great as does a pail of dated chicken or various other meat by-products left out in the sun for several weeks.

- Another trick is to smear lard, cooking grease or even peanut butter on several nearby tree trunks to help "steer" the bear towards the bait station. An incoming bear goes from one tree to the next until he "stumbles" upon your cache of goodies. Even a burlap bag soaked in molasses and then spread between branches where it can catch the evening breezes has been known to attract bears to an ambush site.

- One of the best attractors, however, is a grease pad. Peanut oil, discarded chicken fryer grease or even molasses can be spread upon the ground around the bait site. As bears come to dine, they invariably get the oil or grease on their fur and feet. When they leave and go where bears go, they can't help but leave a scent trail behind that other bears often find irresistible. This is a good way to get multiple bears on a bait station.

- What baits work best? I've been in camp where dog food, vegetables, apples and even popcorn dripping in maple syrup or honey have all been used successfully. Over the years, however, fresh meat seems to work the best, especially if the bait is also laced with sweets such as dated pastries, marshmallows, candy bars and raw honey. Experiment and see what the local bears prefer; then make sure they have plenty of it to chow down on when you are not around.

- Whenever possible, establish a "staging area" for yourself. This will allow you to check the bait site from afar using a pair of binoculars without stinking up the site with your stench. This also helps keep unwanted noise to a minimum.

- Bears quickly adjust to baiting routines. The sound of your truck, for example, often tells a bear camped out on the bait site that you have again arrived to bring him more food. As soon as you leave, he may very well hit the bait, often in the middle of the day, when you are not around. More on this in the chapter on "Strategies for Finicky Bears."

HOT FALL BAITING SITES

Despite all the foods available in the spring, black bears do not begin to put on serious weight until the summer berry crops ripen. If still available in early fall, you will find bears in meadows, clear-cuts and open hillsides

Preferred fall food sources include abandoned apple orchards and cultivated oat fields.

feeding on strawberries, blueberries, service berries, raspberries, blackberries, dogwood, wild plums and hawthorn.

Forget last spring's bait stations near water unless there is a favorite fall food available nearby. If you are going to bait in the fall, you must bait near preferred fall food sources. And be aware that the more fall food available, the more difficult it will be to get a bear to come to your station. Of course, if fall foods are scarce, your bait station could be the hit of the area. Here are some additional tips for the fall:

- Droppings mixed with wild seeds should give you clues as to where the bears might be congregating.
- Look for broken plant stems and bear trails littered with droppings in the better feeding areas.
- Glass the shadows and edges of openings early in the morning and again late in the afternoon for feeding bruins. A bait set-up here could be "claimed" overnight.
- Cherries are another early-fall favorite. Look for scat around the base of the tree, claw marks on the trunk and "bear nests" in the uppermost branches. Once the cherries are gone, the bears will feed elsewhere.
- From mid to late fall, bears will concentrate on standing farm crops such as corn, oats and apples as well as beechnuts and acorns in the big woods. As long as there is sufficient food available, many of the bigger bears will remain active. It is not uncommon to see large bear tracks in six inches of snow.

DEBUGGING THE BUGS

Biting insects like mosquitoes, gnats, no-see-ums and, of course, the worst of the lot, the dreaded black fly, flourish in bear country—especially in eastern Canada where black flies are as much a part of growing up as ice hockey. Nonetheless, that does not mean you have to let the little buggers ruin a night on stand. If you are ready for them, they can actually add a bit of spice to a long evening in the bush.

Keep in mind that bears are more often on the move when the bugs are out in full force, so most experienced spring bear hunters welcome the buzzing and whining of hordes of insects. In fact, the bugs seem to torment bears to no end, zeroing in on tender areas around the eyes, ears and anus at will, making their lives about as miserable as one can imagine. It is not uncommon, therefore, to see a bear approach a bait site with a cloud of blood-sucking insects hovering around his face and rear end like a bunch of screaming kids circling an ice cream truck on a hot summer day. Here are some debugging tips:

- Learn to spray all exposed skin, including face, neck, ears, forearms, wrists, hands and legs with DEET. This stuff works hard to keep bugs at bay,

Whoever invented DEET has a seat in heaven, despite what he or she may have done with the rest of his or her life!

but you may need to re-spray the same areas after a couple of hours.

- Using electrician's tape, secure pant cuffs and shirtsleeves. Any area not snugly bound is an open invitation for a free meal. No tipping!
- Head nets are quite necessary if the clouds of insects become so thick you can't breath without inhaling a few dozen of the little, uh, buggers. Be sure to tape down the "tail" of the head net, too.
- Bug jackets and pants work great. Spray DEET on them for extra protection. They also help keep you warm after the sun goes down.
- If you don't have a bug-proof outfit, wear long johns under your camouflage. This will help stop mosquitoes from "drilling" through the fabric.

New bear hunters sometimes scoff at the above precautions. They don't realize that even a square inch of bare skin can invite hundreds of black flies in for a nice meal. They can and will dine at will, leaving you a bloody mess by evening's end.

One year "Steve," a local bowhunter, booked his first ever black bear hunt in Ontario. Despite good advice to the contrary, "Steve" wore jeans with a button fly and refused to wear a head net or to tape those jeans to his rubber boots. Well, you guessed it. He literally got chewed

Pick a spot, come to full draw, smooth release and good follow through: The Moment of Truth.

The near foreleg is fully extended and the bear is facing away. And he is a 500-pounder, too. Shoot!

alive from head to toe, and when a bear finally did show up just around nightfall, "Steve" was so out of sorts he couldn't draw his bow. Then, to make matters worse, on the way back to camp, he drank water from a near-by lake—again against local advice—and contracted Giagardi, better known as "beaver fever," and spent the rest of the week with a roll of toilet paper stuffed in his jacket pocket.

The moral of this story is that it doesn't pay to be a know-it-all. Pack a head net, plenty of DEET and a roll of electrician's tape into your daypack. And then don't drink the water. Ever.

TAKING THE SHOT

Two of the advantages of shooting bears over bait are that you generally have ample time to size up the ani-

mal, and then you usually have the luxury of waiting for the perfect, one-shot kill. If you have set up with a modern rifle or muzzleloader some distance from the bait site, then you can use a rest and make the shot impersonal.

All bets are off, however, when you are out on a limb near the bait barrel or hiding behind some brush at ground zero. This is where an unwanted noise or an involuntary movement can send a big bear packing. Indeed, this is where even an experienced big-game hunter can get "bear fever" and blow the shot of a lifetime.

If a bear spots you sitting in your stand, for example, curiosity may get the better of him and he will come over for a closer look-see. One of the real thrills of bear hunting is having a 400-pound boar march over to the tree you are sitting in, stand up and go "woof, woof" in your face. If that doesn't kick-start your imagination, you either have nerves of steel or you passed out on the first "woof."

Over the years I have had several bears climb up the

tree towards me, mostly out of curiosity. Usually the bear will shin back down the trunk, but a couple of times, I have had to yell at him when he got too close (okay, so I lost my nerve!). Once I even had to kick my boot at his snoot to get him to go away. Generally, however, if you just sit still, the bear will soon be satisfied you are harmless and shuffle over to the bait barrel.

New bear hunters often get the jitters as a bear makes his final approach to the bait site. If your leg starts to hop about then like a rabbit on the run, your best defense is to decide not to take the shot. You will be surprised how cool, calm and collected you can be when there is no pressure to shoot. Just sit back, relax and enjoy the show! The bear may leave, but if not disturbed, he is more than likely to return. And when he does, he will be more relaxed and so will you—maybe even enough to make the shot.

One of the secrets to shooting a big bear at a bait site, be it with modern firearm, muzzleloader or archery tackle, is to be sitting stone-still facing the bait with weapon in hand. Wait patiently for the bear to relax and look away or put his head in the barrel or just lay down and become preoccupied with eating. If you can keep your wits about you, this is the time to pick a small spot at which to shoot, raise your weapon, take careful aim—and shoot.

SHOOTING FISH IN A BARREL, OR JUST A BARREL OF FUN?

It was still dark when Charley walked me to my treestand. Built six feet off the ground, the rickety wooden platform overlooked a beaver dam and a pile of dead suckers, both only 10 yards distant.

"The dam is littered with bear tracks," whispered Charley as he handed me my bow, "and the bait pile has been hit several times. You'll have an easy shot if he shows up. By the way, I suspect this bear has been hitting the bait as soon as the truck departs, so get ready and stay alert. We'll pick you up in four hours. Good luck!"

I tightened my safety belt, sat down and fumbled an arrow out of the quiver. Only then did I dare lean back onto the tree and try to relax a bit. This was a tough assignment, however, as I couldn't see my hand in front of my face, and I knew I was going to be alone in the darkness for quite some time. Pink light was still over an hour away.

Then sure enough, as soon as the drone of Charley's 4x4 faded into the Canadian darkness, a twig snapped in the darkness a few yards behind the stand. Then the crack of another twig split the air, and then another. My heart was racing as the creature neared my not-so-lofty perch before passing unseen underneath my platform. I struggled to control my breathing, terrified the bear would discover my quivering frame a few feet above and slap me out of the treestand. The tension in the air was so thick you could cut it with an axe.

Then all was quiet and remained so until first light. It was then that I learned that the "bear" I heard earlier was probably one of the many snowshoe rabbits hopping about the fringes of the beaver pond that morning.

It didn't matter all that much, however. My first bear hunt was a blast, and I was hooked on bow hunting bruins from that moment on.

Back then, bear hunting over bait was not as controversial as it is today. Due to the misguided actions by left-wing, anti-hunters, the non-hunting voting public has been lied to about the "bear" facts time and time again in order to close seasons. "Bear hunting over bait is simply not right," they say. "The bears don't stand a chance." Indeed, their propaganda played a prominent role in convincing Ontario Premier Snobelen to end the spring bear season back in January 1999.

According to Snobelen's news release faxed to my office that month, "Many people have told us that the way the hunt is conducted is unacceptable. We have reviewed current practices and considered modifications; but none provide assurance that young bears and their mothers would be protected as they emerge from their dens in the spring. Stopping the hunt is the only protection for the animals."

Indeed, the thought of one cub dying as a result of hunting was unacceptable to the minister—regardless of the social/biological/economic implications. In fact, the decision to close the bear season jeopardized 40 million tourist dollars, including $2.2 million from spring bear license sales earmarked for hunting and fishing programs.

The minister did get solid biological information on bear hunting from several sources. He was also aware that Ontario's bear population, the third highest in North America, remains healthy and that harvest figures were well within sustainable guidelines. He was also aware that there had only been a couple of cases where it was reported a hunter shot a sow with cubs, proof that nearly all bear hunters condemn the practice. He also knew that hundreds and hundreds of cubs die each year from natural causes as well as predation, accidents, disease and cannibalism. Indeed, the issue was not biology or ethics. It was then and still is a social issue.

WESTERN BEAR HUNTING

But some hunters also believe that there is something inherently unfair about hunting bears over bait. "It just seems too easy to me," a Montana bowhunter once told me at an archery show, "like shooting fish in a barrel. After all, everybody knows that bears are suckers for donuts and dead fish. All you have to do to get a shot is wait until a hungry bear walks close to your food pile. I don't see the sport in that."

Of course, my Montana friend did think it was okay to set up a treestand near a farmer's apple orchard or along the edge of a cornfield for whitetails. "Two good places to arrow a big buck," he told me with sly confidence. What is so different then about hunting bears over bait I asked him? Planted cornfields and cultivated apple orchards are both "unnatural" man-made food sources that attract big-game animals.

My friend's preferred method for taking a bear with a bow and arrow was to spot-and-stalk them. In the spring, you can glass clear-cuts and walk Forest Service maintenance roads in the hopes of catching a bruin flat-footed as he searches about for the season's first greenery. Similarly, you can glass chutes and open basins in the fall for bears gorging themselves on gobs and gobs of juicy huckleberries.

Indeed, several of my spot-and-stalk bear hunts in the open West were thrilling. Like the time I tried to put the sneak on a Pope and Young candidate in northwest Montana. The bear just as quickly spotted me, however, and I spent the next hour playing hide and seek with that big bear as my guide watched from an open vantage point high up the mountain. I never did get a shot.

Or like a couple of years ago when bowhunting the open farmland of southern Alberta. Bears here feed near sunset in oat fields much like whitetails feed on alfalfa or beans elsewhere in their range. Most of my attempts ended in failure as one bear after another saw, heard or smelled me before I could work in close enough for a bow shot.

Calling to bears already in sight is another tactic that works in the open western states and provinces. It is amazing how far a bear will travel to take advantage of a prey animal in pain, and how fast he will cover that distance to claim that easy meal. Over the years, my friends and I have called several bears to within close range by blowing wildly on a high-pitched predator call. And each close encounter left us completely exhilarated.

The point is that when hunting black bears in the wide-open spaces, spot-and-stalk as well as calling with a mouth-blown predator call are both productive tactics. You don't need to bait because you can either sneak in on a bear you have already spotted, or catch one feeding and bring him to you by calling.

EASTERN BEAR HUNTING

However, when hunting the thick, mixed spruce-fir forests that range from Alberta and Saskatchewan to Manitoba, Ontario, Quebec and Newfoundland, both of these methods fall short. Why? The thick forest limits visibility to distances often less than 20 yards. Unless you hunt the shorelines of lakes and rivers, you are not going to get an opportunity to see many bears going about their everyday business.

And secondly, overland travel through the bush is quite noisy. In fact, it is almost impossible to walk up on a "bush" bear in the wild. Their hearing is excel-lent, and they will be gone well before you arrive on the scene. This fact is why baiting is so appealing in most of Canada—your chances of seeing a bear without baiting are somewhere between slim and none.

But baiting also has other advantages. For example, it gives the hunter the time to be selective in not only what animal he shoots, but also when to shoot at that animal. Thus, killing sows with young bears can easily be avoided.

Indeed, even though it is already illegal to shoot lactating females, females with cubs or solitary cubs all across their range, Ontario game officials admitted to Premier Snobelen that there had only been one conviction in the recent past out of two arrests. This proves that bear hunters hunting over bait in Ontario are quite careful.

One of the more difficult aspects of bear hunting is field judging the size of a bear. At first glance, ALL bears look big. You will soon find out that it takes practice and plenty of experience to accurately judge the live weight of a black bear. Even then, it can be difficult to tell the difference between a young 200-pound male and a 450-pound mature boar.

A Saskatchewan trapper once told me that after hauling the 700 bears he had legally trapped in his lifetime, he was pretty good at guessing the live weight of any bear if he could slide it into a wheelbarrow. If he couldn't do that, then "it was anybody's guess how big the bear really was."

This task can be all the more difficult if you only have a limited view of the bear or a few precious seconds to make up your mind before you shoot. Bowhunting over bait, however, can generally give you all the time you need to make certain of the age and sex of the bear in front of you.

The other plus to hunting bruins over bait is that you can wait for the perfect 15-20 yard broadside or quartering-away shot before releasing an arrow. In fact, bowhunters can "crib" their bait sites with logs, stumps, brush and the like to force a bear into a high percentage opportunity. This reduces the probability of a poor hit and helps keep recovery rates high.

In my view, the real sport to bait hunting bruins begins the first day of the hunt. This is when I cruise the bait stations looking for the subtle clues of trophy bear activity. Mature bruins are almost always males, and they are bigger and behave differently around a bait station than sows and subordinate boars.

With time and experience, a good bear hunter should be able to read the scuffed-up leaves, crushed vegetation, and the location of scat near a bait site much like a trout fisherman reads the water on a stream. In essence, he should be able to tell you the size, sex and color phase of the bear visiting the station, how often he visits, when he is likely to return and how he enters the site. While some bears sneak in, others will walk right in as if they own the place or wait for you to leave before they stroll in for a meal.

Whenever I hear a bowhunter pooh-pooh eastern bear hunting, it is obvious he has had little experience with black bears, and as a result has little respect for their cunning. Trappers and other outdoorsmen that frequent the North Woods will tell you that there is only one animal smarter than a black bear in the bush, and that is a wolf.

"Cautious Cal" is a case in point.

I almost didn't see him. In fact, if I hadn't casually glanced off to my right that evening, I wouldn't have known something big was lurking in the shadows. It would take another 15 minutes of agonizing searching, however, before I could confirm my suspicions and size him up proper.

It was obvious the 550-pound boar had been there before. He padded across the beaver dam without concern and was now cautiously approaching the bait under a crosswind. I guess that's what made him so nervous. He couldn't get the wind in his favor without exposing himself to the open forest.

Time after time I watched as the Pope-and-Young bruin sneaked up on the pile of donuts and honey only to turn sharply away at the last minute to hide in the dense undergrowth. With each approach, however, he was able to work his way in closer and closer until, eventually, he gathered up enough courage to step into the opening and take a few laps of honey. Satisfied all was safe, he then turned slightly away from me for a few seconds and began gorging himself on the pile of sweets.

That's when I should have taken my shot. I picked a spot behind the bruin's near shoulder, but did not bring my High Country Extreme to full draw. I held, still hoping to get a better angle on a more relaxed bruin. But big bears do not get big by being stupid. I don't know if he caught a slight breeze or heard my heart pounding in my chest. Whatever it was, he sensed danger, and in the blink of an eye, sprang for cover, never to be seen again.

Now who said bowhunting bears over bait is like shooting fish in a barrel?

Spring vs. Fall: Which is the Best Time to Hunt Bruins?

Spring may be popular with many hunters, but given my druthers,
I'll pick a frosty fall morning every time!

The bear left Idaho and slipped into Montana just prior to midnight and then rested in the alders along a dry creek bed a short distance from the border. He stayed there until an hour or so before pink light and then waddled out into the open to feed on the huckleberries that grew in thick patches up and down the basin.

The boar moved from one bush to the next, stripping off several mouthfuls of purple fruit with simple abandon until he reached the rim of the canyon. There he stopped briefly, tested the wind, and then without further hesitation, began slowly working his way back down the hill towards the dry creek bed.

I guess that's when Tim first spotted him. The bruin looked like a tiny black dot on the distant hillside, but Tim immediately recognized that small speck as a bear, and swung his 8X10 Swarovski's up to his face for a closer look.

As Tim studied that speck, I dismounted in a frantic effort to glimpse the bruin for myself. I squinted and looked everywhere, but my efforts were to no avail for my "back-east" eyes could see nothing through my binoculars save empty landscape. In fact, the harder I looked, the more I was convinced I needed a check-up because by now everybody saw the 500-pounder except me. Suddenly, I spotted some movement a quarter mile away as the bruin stepped around some boulders and then padded across the hillside towards another patch of fat huckleberries.

"He's a good bear," whispered Tim when the bruin strolled out into the open, "but there's no cover left, Bill, for a stalk with a bow. Hal, you can have first crack at him with that 300 Win Mag of yours if you think you can make the shot."

Hal smiled and then looked down the slope towards the black speck. The plan was to have Hal, Leonard, and Tim's son Jon take the horses around the face of Mt. Kento and then edge themselves slowly over the rim of the canyon for a look-see. If they could spot the bear from above, it would be an open shot, perhaps 300 yards, but downhill at a fairly steep angle.

Tim and I settled down to watch the action from a brush-studded spur that ran from the top of the canyon all the way down to the dry creek bed. An hour later, the bruin was still feeding unconcerned when the horses appeared on the opposite rim. Soon Hal, Leonard and Jon were seen working their way down the slope towards a rocky point that jutted out over the canyon. A few moments later a single shot followed quickly by a second rang out across the basin. The bruin bolted a short distance, staggered and then collapsed into a lifeless heap.

THE BEAUTY OF FALL BRUINS

Black bears are pursued in the fall and the spring, but given a choice I'd always opt for an autumn hunt. It's the traditional time to be afield pursing big game, especially black bears. Besides, the sky seems bluer then, and there's a welcome nip in the air.

There's also more action in the autumn—a lot more action! Spring bears are lethargic upon emerging from the den and only travel short distances in search of new grasses or an old winter kill. Sightings at this time of the year are often few and far between.

Autumn bears, on the other hand, are moving about almost constantly during daylight hours in search of high calorie foods. They need to put on enough fat at this time of the year to sustain themselves through the den-

Fall bear camp deep in the Alberta wilderness.

ning period, and in most cases, until various berries ripen the following summer.

It's not uncommon then for bears to congregate around stands of beech, berry patches, abandoned apple orchards and cultivated grain fields where they can gorge themselves before the deep snows come. If you can locate such a food source, your chances of having multiple sightings are very good indeed.

Another reason to pursue bears in the autumn rather than the spring is body size. A bruin on good range is in prime physical condition once winter sets up. In fact, in years of plentiful food, black bears can gain an average of 2.2 pounds a day and can, on occasion, double their weight before it's time to seek out a new den site. That means a good 225-pound spring boar could easily weigh 350 to 400 pounds in September. Now, if you were looking for a wall rug or a life-size mount, which bear would you rather tag?

Of course, some hunters believe that bear hides are more luxurious in the fall than in late May or early June. Now, a hide from a bear just out of hibernation can be thick and luxurious, but it can just as easily be ragged and tattered looking, too. According to my friend Eric Grinnel of Silvertip Outfitters, "Spring bruins tend to rid themselves of their underfur as soon as the warm weather arrives by rubbing their bodies against rocks, roots and rough-barked trees. Autumn bears, however, do not rub their hides. In fact, the colder it gets, the thicker the pelt!"

Another good reason to be afield in the fall rather than the spring is the general lack of biting insects. The first time I bowhunted bears was in the spring many years ago in eastern Canada. I came to camp equipped with a head net and some repellant, but the mosquitoes and black flies nearly carried me away. I learned the value of DEET that year and how to tape my sleeves, pant legs and head net tightly against my body. I never did learn how to scratch without cursing, however.

FALL BRUINS—THE SECRET TO SUCCESS

Most black bears tagged in the fall are taken by hunters in search of other game. Here in the East, the bulk of the bear harvest takes place during the regular big-game season when deer hunters and bruins so often blunder into each other.

Taking a fall bear by design, however, requires more than mere luck; it takes lots of hard work and planning. Come autumn, bears enter a stage called hyperphagia, or excessive eating, where they range far and wide in search of caloric-rich forage. Instinct tells them they must put on enough fat at this time to sustain themselves during the upcoming denning period.

Fall bears will often ignore small scraps of food left by hunters such as small bags of bait positioned in the middle of nowhere and congregate instead near oak hol-

Fall bears can gain 150 or more pounds after emerging from the den.

Spring hides can be badly rubbed. The underfur is the first to go, often coming out in handfuls. Unless diseased, fall bears do not rub their hides.

lows and beech ridges, apples orchards, cultivated grain fields … and berry patches! Indeed, if you can manage to concentrate your hunting efforts near a proven fall food source, your chances of collecting a trophy-size bear are very good.

In western states like Montana and Idaho, it's the huckleberry crop that gets the most attention from the bear population, especially if there has been lots of rain and warm temperatures during the growing season. Ideally, these berries start ripening in the lower elevations around the first of June. As they dry and drop to the ground, others ripen at progressively higher elevations until only the upper basins have sweet berries when the fall hunting season arrives.

The plan then is to get on top of the mountain before methodically glassing the various basins and open slopes for feeding bears. First light and dusk are the best times to be afield, but a good bear can be spotted at almost any time of the day.

We know, too, from experience that bears will keep coming back to a patch of berries as long as the food lasts. We will, therefore, sometimes sit above a berry-laden basin all day if need be until a bear steps out into the open to feed.

Not everybody likes the idea of hunting black bears in the fall, however. Some hunters erroneously believe that hunting bears at this time of the year interferes with other

There is no reason not to take advantage of multi-species hunts; keep your eyes peeled for a big bear while hunting moose, elk or deer.

Many black bears tagged in the fall are targets of opportunity. This is when a deer hunter and a wandering bear blunder into each other at point blank range.

Out West the plan is to get to the top of the ridges before first light and glass open meadows for feeding bears. Plans can go awry, however, if morning fog obscures the landscape.

big-game hunting. Well, nothing could be further from the truth. Your first option is to plan your fall bear hunt as part of a multi-species adventure. For example, a western elk/bear hunt or a Canadian moose/bear hunt can prove doubly rewarding in these hard economic times. Of course, if the moose aren't in rut yet or the elk stopped bugling, you might just run across a bear feeding on a far-away ridge and salvage the trip.

If you want to try your hand at an early autumn bear hunt here in the East, then take a week off in mid-September or early October and head for the hills. You can have a ball without the trip interfering with any of the early archery or regular upcoming deer seasons. In fact, you can toughen your body and sharpen your deer skills by simply giving a fall bear hunt your undivided attention.

The secret to finding bears this early in the year is to key in on emerging food supplies. In New York's Adirondack Mountains, for example, Mark Eddy, a registered guide and outfitter, looks for bear sign near groves of cherry trees and then sets up treestands nearby for his clients.

"The bears will gorge themselves day after day on the ripe cherries," says Eddy, "so your chances are good if you can sneak in and out of the area without traumatizing the bears with your scent or clumsiness. I keep an eye on large stands of wild cherry during the summer, and then as the berries ripen, I revisit the groves looking for fresh claw marks on the tree trunks and 'bear nests' high in the branches for signs of bear feeding activity."

Some of the Adirondack's most famous waterways also have cherry trees growing along the shoreline, so it makes sense to use a canoe to penetrate some of the more remote hot spots. You can still-hunt the groves early in the morning and again late in the afternoon. If the bears are feeding in the grove, you should see, in addition to the claw marks and "bear nests" in the uppermost branches, plenty of scat around the bases of the trees, giving you an indication as to frequency of the visits and the size of the bears.

As the cherries disappear, you will have to go with the flow and seek out other feeding locations. Abandoned apple orchards are always a favorite, followed by stands of other soft mast such as beechnuts and acorns.

In summary, bagging a bruin in the spring is exciting, but a fall hunt offers many advantages not available to you earlier in the year. Me, a horseback hunt in the Rockies with a couple of pals is often reward enough, bear or no bear. But if I can't get out there, I'm just as happy packing my vintage Savage 99, chambered in the venerable 300 Savage, and still-hunting the North Woods for something other than a white-tailed deer. It adds a whole new dimension to the term outdoorsman.

In the East, fall bear hunts are great warm-ups for the upcoming deer season.

Strategies for Finicky Bears

How you ring the dinner bell is what really matters!

Iexpected the bear to come in from my right, the way one had the previous evening, but as the sun set, the forest was exceptionally quiet and nothing was moving. Or so I thought. I heard a small twig snap at the base of my tree and when I looked down, I got the surprise of my life. There, only 8 feet below me, was a huge black bear. How he got there I don't know, but I do know that it was a long 2 minutes before that bruin turned his eyes away from my twitching stomach and walked unafraid towards the bait.

I dared not reach for my bow and hardly had time to resume breathing before the bear grabbed a chunk of chicken and headed back towards my stand. I watched in disbelief as he walked right to the base of my tree before exiting behind me without making a sound. Once he was out of sight, I began to shake so badly I felt I had to hug the tree to stop from falling out—even though I was securely buckled in with a 3-foot-long safety belt.

Five minutes later, I saw the bear approach the bait site again. He took the exact same route as before, but this time he didn't pause at the base of "my" tree. Instead, he padded right over to the bait bag and began chowing down on all kinds of goodies I set out just for him. I watched him feed and bided my time. When the bruin finally presented me with a quartering-away shot, I took careful aim and sent a razor-tipped camo shaft through both lungs.

It has become a rite of spring, I suppose, baiting for black bears. It is especially popular in those states and Canadian provinces where thick swamps, dense brush land and heavily wooded areas make it difficult to pursue these elusive creatures in any other manner. Although bears are truly suckers for leftover foodstuffs, enticing a trophy bruin out of the shadows and then into bow range is no easy matter. Even a reputable outfitter can have a difficult time at it.

The problem seems to lie with the psychology of some black bears. Let me explain. Black bears are almost always hungry and spend most of their waking hours in search of food. Nothing gets by that sniffer of theirs. Absolutely nothing! However, unlike whitetails and other prey animals that bolt at the mere presence of man, a black bear will not necessarily abandon a preferred food source because of human intrusion.

The truth is, a big and brassy bruin would much rather figure out a way to steal your bait when you're not around than go elsewhere for lunch. Thus, as any experienced bear hunter can tell you, getting a big black bear to hit your bait is easy, catching him at it is the hard part. That's why serious trophy hunters generally opt for a 10-day to two-week hunt rather than the standard 5- or 6-day trip. Bad weather and finicky bruins take their toll, and you will often need the extra time to match wits with a cunning old bear. Here are six strategies designed to help you outsmart those tricky trophy bruins of the North Woods.

DOUBLE-TEAM THE BAIT SITE

Remember Ivan Pavlov? He was the Russian physiologist who discovered a phenomenon called the conditioned reflex. Using laboratory dogs, he found that if a stimulus that automatically elicits salivation, such as meat paste, was repeatedly presented to a dog just as a tone sounded, the tone alone would eventually come to elicit the salivation. Even seeing the person who ordinarily brought the food, or hearing his footsteps, also got the dog to salivate.

What has this got to do with bear hunting? Well, bears can quickly become conditioned to the clamor of hunters running a bait line. They learn to associate fresh food with such sounds as a particular truck's engine or noises of people approaching the bait site, much like Pavlov's dogs did to the tone used in the laboratory.

It's understandable then for a hunter to be dropped off at his treestand 4 hours before sunset only to find a bear has already beat him to the bait. That afternoon the

Some hunters would rather chase bears around than fish for spring steelhead or call to hilltop gobblers. Imagine that!

bear heard a familiar truck slow down, stop, a door open and close, and then drive off just like he's heard so many times before at that time of day. These familiar sounds rang his chimes, and he came into the bait expecting dinner. The only problem is he came 4 hours before you arrived on stand.

What can you do? We learned to outsmart the bear by running our bait line earlier in the day and then making lots of noise when we replenished the bait. After a few days, one hunter climbed into his stand during the re-baiting process while the other returned to the truck and drove off. It fooled the bear, and we dragged a nice bruin out of the woods an hour later.

Sometimes, a bear will not come into the bait until he hears a hunter crawl out of his stand, walk to his truck and drive away. I hunted such a bait-wise bear, and we got him to come to the bait one evening by tricking him into believing I had left my stand early.

We put up an additional stand near the bait, and when evening came, my pal and I climbed into our respective stands. A half-hour before darkness, Charley climbed out of his stand, walked to the 4x4 and drove off. He didn't drive 100 yards down the road before the bear strolled into the bait as if he owned it, offering me an easy 15-yard shot.

If you're having a problem catching a bear at the bait, take a second look at your operation. You may have inadvertently conditioned the bruin to your baiting and hunting routines.

MANIPULATE THE BAIT

Running a bait line is much like checking a trap line—you never know what you're going to find until you get there. A hit may be light, meaning a bear is only nibbling on a few choice morsels, or heavy, meaning the bear(s) cleaned you out.

The best-case scenario is to find the bait gone. The last thing you want now is to have the bear go elsewhere to feed, so don't hesitate to generously restock the site. Make sure the bruin is not dragging large chunks of bait off and gnawing on them some distance away. If this is the case, try using smaller morsels that can be readily gobbled up. You want the bear to spend as much time at the bait site as possible.

Light hits are common in the early spring, a time when bears are just leaving their dens. Spring start-up baits should include a stinky "draw" bait, such as a pail of rotten chickens, in addition to a wide variety of fresh meats, vegetables, breads and pastries. You may find bits of grass in their scat, indicating a preference for sedges and green shoots at this time of the year. Nonetheless, replenish the bait by paying close attention to whatever the bear ate. He'll keep coming back as long as you continue to give him what he wants.

Irregular hits are a real challenge to the bear hunter. For example, by using a timer, you discover that your bait

There is always a bear nearby when you are around an active bait station. And like it or not, you are conditioning him to your activities much like Pavlov conditioned his dogs.

is being hit regularly, but at odd hours of the day, say 1:00 P.M. and 6:30 P.M. on two successive afternoons, and then 11:15 A.M. the following morning. You most likely have at least one bear camped out nearby, a bear that waltzes into the bait whenever the urge strikes him. This set-up is good for the bear, bad for you.

It sounds complicated, but the solution is simple. Put as much of the fresh bait as you can into bags or buckets, and haul it out after each hunt. It's a good idea to keep the bruin interested by leaving a few tidbits on the ground, but don't replenish the bait until you return to the site the next evening. If the bear comes to the bait when you're gone, he'll only have a snack to munch on. He'll keep returning though until he learns the main course is not available to him until later in the day. The idea is to "teach" the bear that dinner is served only between certain hours. It may take a few days, but you'll soon have a reliable evening customer.

NOCTURNAL GIANTS

When a bear goes nocturnal, he becomes almost impossible to tag. He knows when you arrive at the bait site, he knows what you smell like and he may even recognize you by your clothing. In short, he has YOU pegged. Still, there are some things you can try.

One trick is to set up another bait upwind and a quarter mile or so away from the present site. The

Irregular hits are a real challenge to the bear hunter.

object is to get the bear interested in an alternate bait site. Restock the bait in the middle of the day and keep the new site clean. Hopefully, the bear will get into the habit of hitting the new site early before waddling over to the old site sometime after dark. You must not hunt this new site until you are sure the bear feels safe at the bait and conditions are right. You will probably only get one chance at the new site.

This strategy can be especially effective when hunting with outfitters who use permanent stands year after year. Black bears have excellent memory and will return year after year to investigate an old bait site. If there is food present, he may just return again and again as long as he is not disturbed. One close call with a human, however, is often all it takes for him to immediately abandon that permanent site, at least during daylight hours, and maybe even for the entire season. There is another lesson here and that is to take the first good shot you have on a jumbo bruin. The bear may only show up once with you in attendance, so shoot when you have the chance!

(Left) When a bear goes nocturnal, try setting up another bait station upwind and at least 400 yards away. (Bottom) Challenge a boar's supremacy by depositing another bear's scat near the bait station.

It may take erecting a second or even a third treestand to outwit a bait-wise bruin.

Every serious bear hunter should have the fixings for a honey burn in his "possibles bag."

SECOND-GUESSING TROUBLESOME BRUINS

A few years ago, I got a call from an old friend who had some big bears coming into a string of well-established baits. He tagged a good one his first night aloft, and after talking a bit, he invited me out for a quick 3-day black bear hunt (okay, I begged him!).

One of the bruins was a 300-pound, bait-wise son-of-a-gun who was getting even fatter at my friend's expense. No matter what was tried, Brassy Boy would always circle the stand before committing himself to the bait. If the bear smelled a human at the site, he would melt back into the darkness, abandoning the bait site for the night. His pie-plate-size tracks were readily visible the next morning, giving us his exact approach route.

It wasn't until well after the hunt did I realize what we should have tried. A small portable stand could have been erected downwind of Brassy Boy's approach path. This would have allowed us a shot at him earlier in the evening as he wandered around behind the bait site waiting for darkness to fall. Or we could have double-teamed the bait site with one hunter exiting a half-hour or so before dark while the other remained positioned in the small portable. Or we could have simply waited on the ground downwind of the bear's entrance route and arrowed him after he walked past us. Hindsight is always 20-20, but that's how we learn sometimes, too.

Scent sticks are easier to transport and set up than a honey burn, and the odor of "12 Miles of Dead Fish" will certainly get any nearby bear's attention.

TELL HIM HE'S NOT THE BOSS

Trophy bears often leave piles of scat scattered in and around the bait site and especially on entrance and exit trails. It seems the bigger the boar, the larger the scat, both in diameter and total amount. As I mentioned earlier, it seems big bears—those that are approaching Boone & Crockett status—deposit their scat purposely and strategically around a favored food supply as a territorial marker and as a warning against trespass to other boars.

The presence of scat tells you a big bear is visiting the bait, but why doesn't he drop by when you are around? There are many possible reasons, including the fact that he may have hooked up with a sow near estrous. Sometimes, however, he is well fed and just wants to keep tabs on his other food sources.

A case in point was the year I sat over a bait for over a week waiting for the bear that left the large piles of strategically deposited scat nearby to show up. One evening I finally caught a glimpse of him padding up and down the entrance and exit trails, stopping often to test the wind and sniff the ground-level vegetation. Maybe he was scent checking the trails for intruders. In any event, even though the wind was in my favor, the bear never did approach the bait barrel. What could I

have done to entice the bear to come in a little closer?

A few years ago I hunted in New Brunswick with Brian MacVicar and his partner, Jim Parker of Atlantic Adventures. Their solution to the problem was both unique and pragmatic. They got the boss boar fired up by simply depositing another bear's scat on the entrance and exit trails.

"Take a shovel and scoop up the poop from another area," MacVicar and Parker told me, "and then deposit it around the bait site in a manner similar to what another boar might do. Now, obviously, you can't always tell if these droppings are from a male, but even scat from a strange bear, one not living in the immediate vicinity, seems to have a challenging effect on a dominant boar. Obviously, however, if you can doctor up the bait site with droppings from another male bear, the results will be more rewarding!"

MacVicar and Parker claim success with this technique. It certainly had piqued my imagination. Indeed, this is definitely a form of bear communication that needs further research!

THE LAST STRAW

Sometimes, no matter what you do, the bear just isn't going to show himself when you're around. Maybe there's an ample supply of natural food nearby, or maybe he's just finicky. Or maybe he knows darn well you're after his hide! Whatever the reason, your ace in the hole in these situations is a honey burn.

Bears love honey and will go to great extremes to get it—even if they have never tasted it before! If you have a bear camped out near the bait and the bear hasn't been fooled by a honey burn before, I can't imagine you NOT having any action as long as you are careful. The first time we tried this, we took three Ontario bears in two successive nights. Now, I always have the makings of a honey burn with me to sucker punch a wary bruin.

A honey burn is a one-man operation that is easy to set up. First, you'll need a one burner stove. We made our own out of a large canister of "canned heat" and two discarded soup cans, but a Coleman stove will also do the trick. Next, get some store-bought honey. A pint is sufficient for each burn.

Basically, there are two kinds of honey burns. A "hot" burn quickly incinerates the honey into thick clouds of white to black smoke, while a "slow" burn gently boils the honey away into clear vapors. In addition to attracting hungry bruins, both types of burns also work well as cover-up scents, with the "slow" burn lasting longer in this regard.

Like hunting from a new treestand, your first attempt will usually produce the best results. Be sure to experiment with your heat source and varying amounts of honey before you try your honey burn out at the bait site. You don't want to take a chance of spooking your bear

You can't fool a bear's sniffer, but you can overpower him with honey to see if he drops his guard.

by getting in and out of your tree stand to make necessary adjustments. The bear could come in at any time, so be on constant alert!

One year, we tried three honey burns on three different bait sites in one night and arrowed three bears within an hour of firing up the burners. The best evenings seem to be those that are damp with humidity or heavy fog. The sweet clouds seem to drift ever so slowly through the bush, depositing gobs of scent everywhere. The bears can't seem to resist the cloying draw and approach the site early in the evening.

As I mentioned earlier, a honey burn can also be used to help cover up your scent. I say help because I don't believe you can completely fool a bear's sniffer under any circumstances. You can, however, smother him with the sweet stuff to see if he drops his guard.

One year, I had the wind change on me after I had climbed aloft over a hot bait set-up. My scent began to drift towards the swamp where we suspected the bear was bedded during daylight hours. Rather than give up the stand, I lit a honey burn two hours before sunset and watched as the cloud of sweet smoke drifted slowly towards the swamp. Twenty minutes or so later, a twig snapped in the swamp telling me the bear was on his way, and sure enough, a patch of black fur soon appeared in the brush off to my right. The bear wasted little time before coming straight to the pot of honey as if he was on a string, giving me plenty of time to come to full draw and put an arrow through both of his lungs.

What can you do if honey is scarce? Improvise! Bacon burns have long been known to attract bruins, as have grease burns. You can also try burning "12 Miles of Dead Fish," a commercial scent stick from Deer Quest LTD, that many bear hunters rave about. You just light it, slide it into a plastic bucket that comes with the packet of scent sticks, and like a honey burn, the scent wafts through the brush, permeating every nook and cranny with its "fishy" odors. If there is a bear around, and the wind is right, he should come in to investigate.

So, there you have it. Six strategies designed to help you bag North America's number two big-game animal. As you can see, he's the master of cat and mouse games, and he is well adapted to the ways of humans. And best of all, he's getting better at it all the time. Now, who says hunting black bears over bait is easy?

Calling Black Bears— It's a Hoot!

There's more than one way to get a bear to sit down in your lap!

There's one, said Ken, "up along the edge of the clear-cut. He's feeding in the shadows right below that old snag. Can you see him?" I adjusted my 8x10 Swarovski's, and suddenly a fat bruin materialized right in front of me. It was a chocolate bear, probably a boar, weighing around 200 pounds. We watched with fascination as the bruin appeared, disappeared and then reappeared in the waist-high undergrowth. After 10 minutes of glassing, we agreed the bruin's preoccupation with the season's last berries made him an excellent candidate for a bow and arrow stalk.

Ken Robins of Whatshan Outfitters and I had been bow hunting for mule deer in the high country, but an early winter storm had dumped snow and then freezing rain on our hunting grounds, making it impossible to put the sneak on a trophy buck. Since I also toted a bear tag, we decided to drop below the snow line and look for an autumn bruin gorging himself on the season's last berries prior to denning. As it turned out, this was one of nearly a dozen bears we spotted in various clear-cuts and natural openings those last few days of the hunt.

I took one last look at that chocolate boar, smeared on some face cream and within minutes, Ken and I were putting the sneak on that bruin. Just about the time we halved the distance, however, the bear stood up and looked over in our direction. We weren't sure he had spotted us, but it was obvious the stalk was not going to be a cakewalk. This bruin was feeding on red alert!

That's when I decided to try one of Wayne Carlton's predator calls. I nocked an arrow, got into position and started a series of loud, painful squeals hoping to entice the bear into bow range. Much to our surprise, the bear charged us before the first note left the valley. There was no doubt this hungry bruin was looking for an easy meal, and by the look on his face, he thought we were it!

I ran out of wind when the bear was about 40 yards away. I was wrong in thinking the bruin would continue in our direction, however. He simply stopped running, turned and walked away towards the dark timber.

"Hit it again," Ken whispered, "before he leaves the cut." I raised the pitch and started wailing again, but this time the bear began circling our position. When he passed behind some cover at 25 yards, I tossed the call back a few yards to Ken and prepared for the shot. Ken kept wailing as the bear, with ears pinned back and a mouth fool of drool, closed the distance to 12 yards. Unfortunately, he came straight at me with head held low and then stopped. I didn't have a clean shot.

After a long minute, Ken threw his cowboy hat at the bruin and then began waiving his arms and yelling at him. It took a few seconds for the bear to realize the ruse before he woofed and struck straight out for the dark timber, his rippling body telling us he was a much bigger bear than what we had first imagined. To have a large predator that close was, as Ken said later when we relived the incident over toasted sandwiches and coffee, quite a hoot!

Indeed, calling black bears can spice up any hunt, and if done properly, can greatly increase your chances of filling a tag. My pal Bob Robb, who now lives in Valdez, Alaska, is also a firm believer in the technique.

"It's best to spot the bear first," says Robb, "which makes the wide open spaces out West and in Alaska ideal for calling. Under these circumstances, I like to first glass in the early morning and again later in the afternoon from a good vantage point. Once a bear is located, I quietly work my way to within a hundred yards or so of the bear before trying to entice him with a squealing rabbit predator call.

"Some bears may completely ignore you while others may high-tail it to safety right after the first note. I've

A large bear will come to a predator call with one thing on his mind—an easy meal.

found the best candidates to be lone boars. A big old male may charge straight in or circle to get the wind and then sneak in quietly using terrain features and available ground cover to his advantage. He is fearless, however, and this can be very nerve racking!"

One thing to keep in mind is that bears have short attention spans and will quickly give up the chase if you stop calling too soon. That's another reason why it's best to work your way in as close as possible before you start your sequence—you don't want to run out of breath too soon!

Other calls work, too. A fawn-in-distress is a proven predator call, and I would love to try a moose cow-calf call in such high moose density areas as Newfoundland, where it has been documented that the island's huge bears routinely dine on baby moose—better than 50 percent of the calf crop in some sections!

Even a whitetail grunt tube can be effective under the right conditions. Three years ago, while deer hunting in Saskatchewan with Zane Pickowicz and Mel Johnson of Pierceland Outfitters, I called in what I initially thought was a rutting whitetail buck. To my surprise, however, a sleek 250-pound black bear answered my grunts. Too bad I didn't have a bear tag, or I could have had an easy bow shot at that hungry fall bruin.

My most stunning example of how a bear will respond to a call, however, occurred in Colorado a few years back. I was elk hunting near Montrose with outfitter Bruce Hyatt.

We had located a herd of elk holed up in a creek bottom, and although the bull would answer our calls, he would not leave the safety of that brush-choked hollow to investigate.

Bruce decided to keep the bull interested by staying put and chirping with his cow/calf call while I tried to crawl a hundred yards or so through the alders to the creek bottom in the hopes of getting a shot. I was about half way to the creek when I heard what sounded like two elk rapidly working their way through the alders in my direction. I immediately nocked an arrow and dropped to one knee.

Suddenly, a 350 to 400-pound chocolate bear broke into the small clearing 10 yards off to my right. I had a shot, but the bear season didn't open until the next morning. The bruin saw me, and after realizing he had made a big mistake, turned and disappeared back into the alders, leaving me with my heart in my throat.

But I thought I heard TWO elk coming my way? I quickly snapped my head around to my left and to my astonishment saw another 350 to 400-pound chocolate bruin laying down on his belly and staring at me only 8 yards distant, his beady little eyes transfixed on my crouched form. I was terrified! I stood up and let out a hoot as much from fear as anything else, which ran the bruin off.

Keep in mind that a black bear coming to a call believes he is on the threshold of an easy meal. He's

Doe bleats, doe contact grunts, fawn bleats, calf calls and fawn-in-distress calls will also tweak a black bear's predatory instincts.

Boars respond to calls in late spring and early summer. Double your chances by using a quality sow-in-estrous urine.

nothing to fool around with. Indeed, all black bears are potentially dangerous, and one coming to a call is even more so. One tactic to counteract this threat is to carry a 12-gauge shotgun (make sure it's legal to do so) or a large can of pepper spray. Another is to hunt with a partner. Bob Robb likes to sit back-to-back with another bowhunter to lessen the chances of being blindsided by a hungry bruin.

SPRING VS. FALL

When is the best time to try calling black bears? As you might imagine, early spring can be difficult. Bears are just emerging from their dens, and their digestive tracts are not quite up to speed. It doesn't hurt to try calling, however, even over bait. You might just get that big bear to come in a little early.

Blind calling adjacent to new clover patches littered with bear droppings is worth a try, as is calling blind near the snow line, along creek bottoms where new grass has been trampled by feeding bruins, and up and down known spawning streams.

Late spring is a different story. Boars have love in mind then and will wander over several home ranges known to be inhabited by females in search of a sow in heat. Robb likes to face upwind and put out two canisters of James Valley bear scent at this time of the year. If a bruin tries to circle downwind, he'll pick up one of the sow-in-heat lures and follow it in, giving Robb an opportunity at a broadside

Find cover and be ready to shoot before you begin calling. Make sure your finger doesn't nock the arrow off its rest.

You can try calling any time of the day in the fall. There's no rush. Eat and give calling another try later in the afternoon.

bear whose attention has been momentarily diverted away from the squealing.

The best time to call bears, however, is undoubtedly in the fall when they feed voraciously in a frantic effort to gain weight prior to denning. Berry patches and abandoned apple orchards are always good bets, as are stands of mast producing oak, hickory and beech. The presence of scat and tracks should help you pick out the more productive locations under current use.

How do you know it was the call that brought the bear to you and not the mere presence of food? By the bear's body language. A bruin coming into a food source, be it natural or man-made, often shuffles his feet and acts disinterested. He may be very cautious, circling and testing the wind often, knowing full well the site could be dangerous.

He will not, however, come charging in with his head held high looking for an animal in distress. When a dominant bear comes to a call, even if he circles, he does so in an aggressive manner. His ears will be pinned back, his hackles will be raised, and he may very well be slobbering drool all over himself. Remember, all his senses will be riveted on discovering and then killing another animal for food – not to steal a donut from a bait pile or a mouth full of berries from an unprotected berry patch.

Please keep in mind that any shot you get at an aggressive, hungry bruin will probably be close—very close. Three- to 5-yard shots are not unheard of! That's why full camouflage is paramount. Not just your equipment, and not just your head and torso either, but your face, ears, neck and hands must be camouflaged as well. Your clothing should be also be whisper quiet. Washed cotton is okay, but wool is undoubtedly best.

Once you settle in and start calling, keep all movement to a minimum. A black bear's eyes, like those of a whitetail deer, are very sensitive to movement, especially at close range. He may spot you and exit the scene before you know what happened.

WAYNE CARLTON

Wayne Carlton has been experimenting with various calls for more than a decade, and he now believes that a high-pitched predator or diaphragm call is one of the keys to getting a bear to come a-running.

"The first step to successful bear calling," says Carlton, "is to key in on food. In the spring of the year, that may be a winter kill or tender young grass, whereas in the fall, preferred food sources include berries and mast. The point is that to get a bear to respond your call, you must call in an area known to be frequented by bears.

"If you can spot a bear first," adds Carlton, "your chances of success soar to 90 percent. Set up as close to the bear as possible without alarming him. However, like turkey hunting, you want the bear to feel comfortable as he comes to the call. In other words, don't expect a bear to cross a fence or wade a creek to locate the source of the wailing and screaming.

"The third step," says Carlton, "is to call continuously. Not cautiously mind you. You want to sound like a rabbit being torn limb from limb. If the bear falters, you may have to increase the pitch and volume to get him to re-commit.

"Finally," advises Carlton, "keep calling until the bear is within range and in the open where you can get a shot. When you stop calling, the bear may take a few more steps, but it will soon stop and start looking for the source of the squealing. Hopefully, you'll already be at full draw."

One final note: Ken Robins, Bob Robb and Wayne Carlton all quickly point out that a predator call can lure more than a black bear into your lap. Coyotes, mountain lions and bobcats will all respond to the squeals of a predator call, and so will a grizzly bear. So be careful, and good hunting!

When responding to a call, black bears will try and get the wind in their favor and then use vegetation and terrain features to their advantage in their final approach. Unless you team up with a partner, you will probably be faced with a head-on shot, which is no shot at all with a bow. Practice your high-percentage kill shots.

Be aware! Grizzly tracks mean grizzly bears, and grizzly bears will also respond to your predator call!

Still-Hunting, Stalking, Tracking and Running 'em with Dogs

Baiting is not the only way to acquire a bear rug. The tricks you learned around the bait pile can be used elsewhere in your pursuit of *Ursus Americanus.*

STILL-HUNTING

First one twig snapped and then another and another. I immediately dropped to one knee and waited for whatever was out there to step into the light. With a loud crash, a jet-black boar soon broke from the edge of the swamp and waddled into view a mere 40 yards off to my left. He was on a mission it seemed, hell-bent on leaving the safety of the swamp before sundown, and then bolting across a grown over farm field to a cultivated crop of ripe oats some 300 yards distant.

Without taking my eyes off the bear, I pulled an arrow from my quiver and slipped forward, haltingly at first, one step at a time, but then more quickly in a frantic effort to keep pace with the bear. I had to beat him to the clearing without tipping him off to my presence if I had any hopes of skewering him with a broadhead.

My plan almost worked, but the bear, oblivious to my crouched form, was just too fast for me. He broke into the clearing, and without so much as a quick look-see around, padded straight across the field to a small copse of aspen and disappeared from view. Undaunted, I picked up the wind and circled the stand of aspen, hoping to intercept him one more time, but it was not to be. I then hurried over to the nearby oat field and glassed for several minutes before I finally realized the old boar had given me the slip, gliding back into the thick Canadian bush like a big black bird on wings.

Still-hunting black bears with gun or bow is a most difficult task. That's because black bears prefer to skulk in the shadows, relying on their senses to sidestep stinky humans rather than break cover and flee at top speed like deer or elk are prone to do at the first hint of trouble. Indeed, even in areas known to harbor good bear populations, close encounters are rare. A black bear's acute hearing and incredible sniffer are, in most cases, more than enough to keep it from harm's way.

As a result, many black bears are not tagged by guile but rather as targets of opportunity, especially during the regular big-game season when a hunter stumbles onto a trophy boar going about his daily routine. In the Northeast for example, most black bears are shot by hunters seeking racked deer, whereas only a few bears are actually shot by hunters seeking a bear rug. The story is similar in moose country north of the border as well as elk and mule deer hunting out West.

There is one notable exception, however, and that pertains to some deer hunters in the Catskill Mountains in southeastern New York. There is a small cadre of bear hunters here who, on opening morning, will wait at the head of draws and canyons for bears to be pushed out of the lowlands by the pumpkin orange army and uphill into a waiting ambush. It doesn't work all the time, but often enough to keep in mind the next time you hunt the whitetail opener in regions where bears thrive.

Aside from relying on other hunters to push a black bear into you, how can a still-hunter increase his chances of a sighting? You have to still-hunt areas where bears are known to congregate. In the spring, that means sneaking along the edges of new tender greenery, such as that found along power lines, gas lines, other rights-of-way, the periphery of lakes, ponds, rivers, streams and, of course, cover-rich clear-cuts, forest maintenance roads and grassy meadows. Matted down vegetation and piles and piles of scat are good indicators the bears are feeding in the area.

You can also try to intercept a bear in the evening as he leaves his daytime lair. Steep hillsides, thick swamps and high peaks are good places to look for tracks and scat. You can still-hunt along natural travel routes such

More than one eastern deer hunter has come face to face to a black bear while en route to erect his deer stand.

In the spring, look for bears to be feeding in the aspens. These claw scars are old, however.

as spurs and gentle slopes, creek beds and open ridges, too, but keep your ears open! You'll be surprised how noisy undisturbed bears can be as they work their way through the forest. On more than one occasion I thought I had a moose passing by only to see a bear break suddenly from cover knocking down deadfalls, tearing up logs, pulling young plants out by the roots and overturning stones in their seemingly never-ending search for food.

In the fall, still-hunting preferred food supplies can also be rewarding. Old apple orchards, berry patches and wild vineyards laden with fat grapes attract hungry bears, as do standing cornfields and, my favorite, fields of ripening oats. In big wooded areas, a bumper crop of beechnuts, cherries or acorns will draw bears from miles around. And the more bears that congregate around any food source—spring or fall—the better your chances of a close encounter.

SPOT-AND-STALK

Spot-and-stalk is the second most popular method for hunting bears. It is practiced extensively in the western states and provinces were bears can often be detected from great distances. The plan is simple. Get to a high vantage point, sit down, and start glassing open hillsides, clear-cuts, hidden meadows, spawning streams, berry patches and, in the case of farm country, fields of active agriculture for fur balls that seem to move slowly about. First light and last light are both prime times to locate black bears, but a good bear can show himself at almost anytime of the day, spring or fall.

You will need good optics, like those offered by Nikon, Swarovsky, Burris, Leupold, Zeiss and others as well as the patience to study every nook and cranny for hours and hours. Bears out in the open are easy to locate, but a bear feeding or resting in heavy cover is not so easy to pick out. It takes practice and a trained eye to spot these bears.

The fun really begins when that speck you have been wondering about unexpectedly moves. Suddenly, you have to ask yourself a myriad of questions: How big is the bear? Is it alone? Is it a boar? What is it doing? How long will it be there? How can I reach it? How long will it take me to get there? If successful, how will I get it out?

One lesson I learned quickly is that western bears have incredible eyesight. They can spot you moving a mile away and will immediately slip back into the shadows. More than one bear I was trying to put the sneak on escaped unscathed because they saw me moving towards them from several hundred yards away.

"The next problem eastern hunters have on western bears," says California outfitter Jon Kayser of Lost Trail Oufitters, "is shooting across great distances. Most

Spot-and-stalk hunting is the second most popular method of bear hunting.

easterners are comfortable dropping a whitetail in his tracks at 100 yards or less, but out West you can commonly expect shots out to 300 yards and beyond. And that requires a whole new mindset in order to be successful."

Kayser has been in on over 200 bear kills. Here is what he recommends you do for a western spot-and-stalk bear hunt.

- Buy only top-quality equipment. Horses and mountain terrain can be rough on all hunting gear. Keep in mind that the best 4X scope is better than a budget-priced 3-9X.
- Adjust your trigger pull to 3-1/2 pounds. Heavy trigger pulls are known to reduce accuracy.
- Start target practicing two months before your trip by emptying a box of shells once or twice a week from a bench rest. Learn where your bullets hit from 100 to 300 yards.
- Learn how to control your breathing and then learn how to squeeze the trigger.
- Load your gun fully and work the action after each shot. You need to make sure your gun will feed each round, especially if you need a quick second or third shot in the field.
- Let your gun cool before each shot.
- Don't hurry your shot.
- Most good target shooters avoid caffeine 1 to 4 days before each match.

- Don't over oil your gun.
- Practice from sitting and prone hunting positions.
- Practice estimating yardage in 100-yard increments.
- Hunt varmints during the off-season.
- Check the accuracy upon arrival in camp. It's amazing how many guns are off the target after a long flight.
- Hunt at your own pace. Slow your guide down if you can't keep up. A good guide won't take offense. He's acclimated to the territory, and he doesn't want you to exert yourself so much you can't shoot accurately.
- Pick a rest whenever possible.
- Don't shoot if you are breathing heavily.
- High winds are not uncommon in mountain terrain, so study ballistic charts before going afield! For example, a 180-grain Nosler Partition at 3000 fps will drift about 6.5 inches at 300 yards with a 10 mph crosswind; 13 inches at the same distance with a 20 mph crosswind.
- Shooting up and downhill can be tricky. Bullets always impact higher on up or downhill shots. Aim low!
- Gravity is what causes a bullet to drop. When shooting at an angle, the distance a bullet is affected by gravity is less than the measured shooting distance. For example, if you have a 300-yard 45-degree downhill shot, the effect of gravity on the bullet is the same as if you were shooting 210 yards. However, the wind blows on the bullet the full 300 yards!

When putting the sneak on a black bear, never take your eyes off him. He can drop into a gully and disappear in a wink, leaving you wondering where you should take your next step.

Never assume your rifle arrived in camp on target and sighted in.

TRACK 'EM DOWN

One of the unique features that separate black bears from other big game animals is their ability to survive all winter without eating anything. Whether they are "true" hibernators like chipmunks and ground squirrels, which drop their metabolic rates by 90 or more percent and nearly freeze to death, or mere "dormants," whose body temperature rarely drops below 88 degrees, is really a matter of semantics. The fact remains black bears spend up to 6 or more months each year curled up in one position without the need to eat, drink, urinate or defecate.

During this "big sleep," black bears lose 20 to 25 percent of their body weight before emerging from their dens—mature boars first, followed by yearling males, barren sows and then sows with cubs—in time to meet the new growth of spring. In the fall, however, this denning sequence is reversed. That is, the big trophy boars tend to den last. In fact, if there is a bumper mast crop, the old boys may be found feeding right into December.

The late Earl Johnson, a well-known Catskill deer and bear hunter, understood this phenomenon quite well. He trailed a number of late season bears in the snow, catching many of them flat-footed right in their beds. "I'll check known crossings for fresh tracks early in the morning," he once told me when I visited him and his wife Emma at their home in Margaretville,

"especially if we got a few inches of snow overnight. Then I'll follow the trail until I see where the bear has walked back and forth on his own tracks a couple of times for a hundred yards or so. At that point I keep to the high ground and proceed with the utmost of caution. With a little luck, I'll find the bruin in his bed nearby.

"One of the more astonishing discoveries I made while trailing bears in the snow," added Johnson that day, "was the fact that they sometimes bend saplings over, biting them off near the ground, and then build a 'nest' of sorts in the snow by crisscrossing several of those saplings. I believe the reason for this was to stop them from sinking down too far in the deep snow, which could interfere with all three of their primary senses. I also knew that if I found a cold, empty nest, the bear had probably been bedding there for some time. I just got there a little too late."

SENSES

Johnson was obviously an expert woodsman. Not many people can claim they can track a buck down in the snow much less a black bear. Nonetheless, one of the reasons Earl was so successful was that he had a great deal of respect for all three of a bear's primary senses. In fact, not paying proper attention to a bruin's eyes, ears and nose is the main reason so few bears are actually seen in the wild.

Take their sight for instance. Most hunters will tell

you eastern bruins are practically blind, but this is simply not so. A stationary hunter may go unnoticed by a black bear, but ready your gun or bow for a shot, and that bear is gone. Johnson told me a black bear can see an approaching hunter at least as good as a whitetail deer, maybe better. "If you stand still, he may think you are another bear, but once he spots you, he won't take his eyes off you until he is sure you do not represent danger."

Their sense of hearing is also underrated. Bears not only hear well, they are also known to outsmart humans by interpreting man-made noises correctly. For example, bears will key in on such sounds as slamming truck doors and banging bait barrels and will lay low until they hear the doors close again and the truck exit the scene. Only then will they stroll up to the bait for a free meal. Johnson also told me only one of the many bears he sneaked up on didn't know he was there. All the rest were sitting up and looking in his direction when he shot. They heard him coming!

Of course, a bruin's nose is legendary. Jack Smith, a veteran Adirondack outfitter who now runs a trophy bear camp in Manitoba, told me bears can detect natural foods at greater distances than most people realize. "Bears can easily smell ripening apples or a grove of beechnuts a mile or more away," said Jack. "That's why we always check these places out for our hunters in the fall. We know that eventually every bear within twenty miles or so will locate concentrations of mast by simply using their sniffer."

It is no wonder then that a black bear can smell a sloppy hunter. "If you want to get the drop on a bedded bear," Johnson cautioned, "then you have to keep the wind in your favor. There is no use following a bear's tracks in the snow otherwise. He will smell you and then just melt into the underbrush. The worst part is you will never know how close you got before he disappeared!"

If you want to try tracking a big bear down before he dens up for the winter, be ready for a long day afield. Johnson told me that when a bear starts looking for food, and not a bedding site, he can cover a lot of ground in no time flat. Indeed, if you don't think a black bear can walk you into the ground, ask any houndsman!

RUNNING 'EM WITH DOGS

Pursuing bears with dogs is still accepted in some areas, although like baiting, the practice is a favorite target of the anti-hunting groups. You will need to know somebody with a pack of trained hounds, or book with a reputable outfitter, if you want to see a treed bear. You better be in shape, however, as you will soon learn just how far and how fast a toothsome bear can run. The dog hunts I have been on have certainly been grueling events, with bears and hounds taking me deep into some of the most inhospitable terrain available—a race, by the way, that the bear often wins "paws" down!

Some hunters, however, frown on chasing bears with dogs, even though they don't seem to mind hunting cottontails or snowshoe rabbits with a beagle or upland birds with Labradors or pointers. The belief that it is somehow not sporting is just one of several myths that permeate the sport, a fact that does not go unnoticed with the anti-hunting crowd. These false crusaders would love nothing better than to split hunters into two or more camps, a goal they have achieved with great success around some campfires in recent years. Here are some of the myths surrounding bear hunting with dogs. Read them carefully, and then make up your own mind.

1. BEAR DOGS ARE VICIOUS CREATURES

I love this one. I backed up the first time I saw a bear dog on a chain, thinking that if I got too close to those canines, he would tear my arm off and have it for breakfast. However, when Brannon Byrne's Sally jumped in the front seat of the 4x4 with me and licked my face, I realized that this dog was about as vicious as a toy poodle. Sally, all 35 pounds of her, not only chases big bad bears with wild abandon, she also likes to see how far a mountain lion will run before it scrambles up a tree. Sure, some bear dogs are rough and tough, but they are not the bloodthirsty creatures they are so often portrayed to be. Bear hounds are bred to run and catch, but they are good-natured animals and even-tempered. In fact, many of the best bear hounds are timid around people and other animals.

2. DOGS ROUTINELY TEAR CORNERED BEARS TO SHREDS

A good pack of dogs, if they can indeed catch up to a black bear, will keep the bear at bay with special barks that the dogs' owners instantly interpret as "We've done our job; now come and get him."

Dogs will nip at the bear at every opportunity, but even a 100-pound bear can take a pack of dogs if he wants to. The hounds are not afraid of the bear, but the bear is afraid of the dogs—at least initially—and that's why the chase takes place. As a black bear matures, however, he learns the dogs are not the threat he first thought they were, and he stops running.

During the chase, the dogs will try to bite the bear on the rump and will often succeed, but with all that hide and fat, the bite never results in a serious wound. When bears fight each other, they bite harder and more viciously than a dog, especially the mature boars! The fact

Jon Kayser knows bears and bear hunting. Read his tips twice.

Shooting at sharp angles is touchy. The distance a bullet is affected by gravity is less than the measured shooting distance.

of the matter is a bear dog could not kill a black bear if it wanted to—even if its very life depended on it!

3. MOST BEAR DOGS ARE KILLED OR SEVERELY MAIMED BY BLACK BEARS

Let's remember that this chase has probably been going on since the dawn of time, whenever dogs and bears bumped into each other in the wilds. Yes, some dogs get torn up, some even die, but not very often. In fact, rarely does a dog even get bitten, maybe one in 50 or 60 chases.

Keep in mind that economically it doesn't make much sense to train a dog to run bears and then let it get maimed by a bear's teeth and claws. Good bear dogs learn fast to keep their distance!

If a dog is seriously wounded, it is usually due to hunter error. When the bear is cornered or treed, the outfitter should tie up the dogs before any shooting takes place. This gives the hunter plenty of time to size up the animal before taking a good clean shot. If the dogs are not tied down and the hunter blows the shot, the dogs will jump into the fracas, and the wounded bear will retaliate against the dogs.

Earl Johnson earned his reputation as a true outdoorsman the old fashioned way—persistence, patience and plenty of hard work.

4. ONCE A DOG PICKS UP THE SCENT, THE BEAR IS DOOMED

Like a rabbit being chased by a barking beagle, a bear will use a lot of tricks to elude a pack of dogs. A bear on the run, for example, will cross streams, climb mountains, circle about on its own trail, seek out thick jungles of impenetrable cover and even scatter the dogs with a false charge or two!

Independent houndsman Brannon Byrne, who has been running bears and cats with Plotts and Walkers ever since he was a pup himself, has "caught" hundreds of black bears by running a pack of dogs. "Many bears will stay out in front of the dogs and will never be seen by anybody," says Byrne. "If a mature bear decides he does not want to be caught, he will simply out-walk the dogs. That's right, not out-run, but keep walking until the dogs become physically run-down.

"Remember they are barking and baying and using up energy while the bear just keeps plodding along using vegetation and terrain features to his advantage. Big old boars are smart and have in many cases been run by dogs before. They are bigger and stronger than the dogs, and each one knows where he is going. He will stop and rest at times, letting the dogs jump around and bark, but eventually he gets going again and simply out-lasts the hounds, walking them right into the ground."

Bryne's best year was in 2003 when his pack of hounds cornered four mature boars that tipped the scales over 500 pounds, two of those going 625 and 650 pounds. These best two had Boone and Crockett skulls, and at press time, were thought to be in the top five of

A black bear's sense of hearing is grossly underrated.

California bear country: rugged, steep and teeming with gargantuan bruins.

the California record book. "These old boars are almost unkillable," says Bryne. "You have to be a good hunter, be in good shape and know the surrounding terrain like the back of your hand. Then you must get ahead of the bear and cut him off 'at the pass,' which is rarely an easy task."

Of course, you don't have to shoot the bear once you have him cornered or treed. Like fly fishing on your favorite stream, bear hunting with good dogs allows you to practice "catch and release" every time afield; only in this version, both the dogs and the bear are smarter for the encounter. A lot smarter!

RADIO TELEMETRY COLLARS

Anti-hunters often claim the use of electronic tracking devices gives an unfair advantage to the hunter. These are the same people, by the way, that decry the use of fish finders, compound bows and other hi-tech advancements. "The real purpose of radio collars is to help you hear the dogs," says Bryne. "When the pack drops into a ravine or goes behind a hill, their barks are no longer audible. With the radio collar, however, you can relocate the pack by climbing onto a ridge or going around the mountain. The beeping will only give you the general direction of the pack, however. It is not a G.P.S. unit. In other words, the radio collars tell you which way they went, not their exact position. Keep in mind that the race is fluid, and as it unfolds, there could be five, ten or even fifteen miles separating you and the dogs.

"Radio collars are most useful when the dog has quit the race and is no longer barking," adds Byrne. "These dogs generally start walking on the first road they come across. If the dog is fitted with a radio collar, then the retrieval rate is cut in half, reducing the likelihood the dog will get hit by a passing motorist."

As you can see, bear hunting with dogs is not the mean and ugly sport so often portrayed by the anti-hunting zealots. It is, in fact, a truckload of fun, and if you like dogs or bears and have not yet booked a hunt, then you are missing out on one heck of a good time!

The baying of the hounds is music to every houndsman's ears.

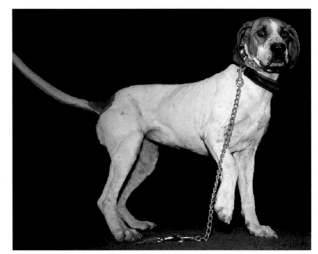

Most dogs that chase bears are about as vicious to humans as toy poodles.

Radio collars and tracking devices help the houndsman keep tabs on his dogs. They are not GPS units.

When a pack of dogs drops into a canyon or goes behind a hill, their voices become inaudible.

The Magnificent Seven

Close encounters with tooth and claw!

Bowhunting black bears can be dangerous. And for four very good reasons: They are intelligent, they are agile, they are powerful and they have no soul. Fortunately for us, most bruins avoid man at all costs, which is a major reason why hunting them with a bow and arrow can be so challenging.

Over the past 30 years or so, I've had hundreds of close encounters with black bears. I've had bears walk within inches of my head while I lay awake in my cot and pay me no heed. I've had bears pad up behind me as I was exiting a tree stand and then run like hell when my foot slipped. And I've had bears sneak to within 10 yards of me, stand on their hind legs, look me straight in the eye—and then disappear into the darkness with a loud WOOF! These bears all left me with a racing heart and a story to tell back at camp, but the Magnificent Seven really scared the pudding out of me—and left me questioning my sanity.

TOO CLOSE FOR COMFORT

In my early years, I often hunted bears alone. That's because few bowhunters were willing to give up their fall deer hunt for an outside chance at a bear. Besides, most hunters are afraid of bears—whether they want to admit it or not—and sneaking around a bear's food supply armed only with a bow and arrow was seen by many of my friends as irrefutable evidence of a brain tumor.

One year, I paid an outfitter to run a bait line for me and then took over the chores when I arrived in camp. That spring, one bait in particular seemed to have a better-than-average bear in residence, but there were no trees nearby suitable for a stand. After giving it careful thought, I elected to try to take the bear at ground zero, so I found a place to sit on the ground next to a pile of dirt and waited for the bear to make an appearance.

The bear's evening routine was simple. He would circle the bait an hour or so before sundown, knocking down deadfalls and breaking branches in the process to warn off any intruders. Then he would sneak into the bait with the prevailing wind to his face and chow down.

It was a good strategy, for twice this bear winded me and melted back into the forest. I then decided to wait back in the brush for the bear to circle the bait before sneaking back to the dirt pile when all was quiet for a shot at the bait just before dark.

My strategy was good too, but it backfired. All I had for cover was a thin curtain of brush that shielded me from the bear's approach. I figured the bear would sneak past me very carefully about 15 yards away with all his senses riveted to the pile of goodies I left out for him. What I didn't figure on was the bear using that same curtain of brush to sneak right up to me. In fact, he got so close I could have jabbed him with an arrow!

When he got broadside to me, the wind suddenly changed, sending a snootful of human odor directly to the bear's nostrils. He jerked his head around, and there we were, eyeball-to-eyeball a few scant feet apart! Instead of hightailing it for parts unknown, as I expected him to do, the boar let out a deep growl, pivoted on his rear legs and lunged at me. I about pissed my pants!

But as soon as his front paws hit the ground, the bear did an about-face and beelined it back towards the swamp, bowling over 4-inch fir trees like they were bundles of tinker toys. In retrospect, I probably scared him as much as he scared me, but I wouldn't bet on it.

THE SWAMP BEAR

I think what scared me most about the Swamp Bear was his incredible strength. I poured a half-gallon of honey over a dead stump one morning and returned 2 days later to find the stump ripped out of the ground, roots and all, by some terrible force and all the honey gone. It was obvious this bear took what he wanted, when he wanted it.

I immediately replenished the bait site, and over the next several days, the Swamp Bear returned every other

Are you asleep yet? What was that sound I just heard outside the tent?

evening to chow down on the honey and other sweets I piled next to the stump. On my last trip to the bait site, I found a 5 1/2-inch front pad track and several piles of 2-inch diameter dung placed strategically around the stump. I replenished the site with honey and assorted sweets before hanging a small portable treestand downwind and 15 yards from the pile of pastries. I let the Swamp Bear have his night off and then sneaked into the treestand the following evening.

Ten minutes before dark a small boar nervously worked his way towards the bait site, stopping often to listen and to test the wind. He was very cautious, which was a good thing because the Swamp Bear was on the prowl that evening, and he wanted his honey—all of it.

Just as the small boar was about to lick the stump, he turned around and stood up to face the bush. He seemed to be having an anxiety attack for all he could do was hiss and back up, hiss and back up. He dropped to all fours, turned his back on the bait and then walked briskly into the bush for a few yards. There he stayed, looking over his rump on occasion, hissing and shaking like a leaf in a windstorm.

I suddenly realized the cause for his concern. The Swamp Bear was nearby. I could not see him, but I could hear him breathing, and the air was alive with his presence. The Swamp Bear did not show himself, however, electing to stay near the bait but in the shadows until it got too dark to see.

Now I was stuck. I was hunting alone, so no one was going to come in and shoo the bear away, at least not this

bear. If I made too much noise getting out of my stand, I could spook the Swamp Bear away, and I would never get a shot. If I managed to crawl out of my stand quietly, I might get a second chance, but I sure as hell didn't want to bump into him as I made my exit, either. The Swamp Bear was just too big to fool with.

I elected to descend quietly and then tiptoe back to my 4X4 with all the caution I could muster. I could feel the hair on my neck stand straight up as I eased away from the stump a few inches at a time. I was terrified, and the sounds of the bear breathing nearby were almost too much for me to handle. By the time I got back to my cabin, I was soaked with sweat. Was the Swamp Bear lying next to the bait, or was I imagining everything?

I slept uneasily for a few hours, but at first light I got up and dressed. I had to find out if the Swamp Bear was at the stump that evening. I grabbed an axe (today I would take my 450 Marlin) and sneaked back towards the stump. To my horror, the bait was untouched, but the spot where I thought the Swamp Bear was hiding was all matted down. He had been there all right, and I had tiptoed within a few yards of him as I made my exit!

Why he didn't bolt then I don't know. Nerves of steel I guess, but I never hunted near that stump again. Never.

PENNSYLVANIA MAMA

Several years ago my friends and I took a week off to bow hunt for whitetails near Coudersport, Pennsylvania.

A black bear will sit tight and let you walk by just like a whitetail buck. Think about that the next time you exit your stand in the dark.

Most of us hunt on the ground by choice. Marvin Vought hunts bears at ground zero because he has to. And he loves every minute of it.

Deer sign was plentiful on state game lands, and we were excited about our prospects. One thing we failed to pay attention to, however, was the large numbers of broken branches that appeared in every apple orchard and berry patch we came across. We didn't know it at the time, but there were eight to 10 bears feeding voraciously on the ripe fruit and berries that fall.

Early one morning, I slipped into the thick brush surrounding an abandoned farm field where I had seen some deer feeding the morning before. I began still-hunting uphill and through the maze of golden rod, black berry brambles and apple trees when all of a sudden a 250-pound black bear stood up in front of me—front legs askew, paws bent at the wrist—and woofed!

I was only one step away, close enough to have easily hit the bruin over the head with my bow. I was flabbergasted to say the least, but also thrilled to find myself so close to such a beautiful animal. I can still see the bear's beady brown eyes staring at me with its black coat glistening in the early morning light. Apparently, the bear had been feeding in the old field and was as surprised to see me as I was to see it.

For a long moment, we just stood there looking at each other and then the bear dropped to all fours and disappeared off to my left in the brush. I then heard a

Big boars don't like to be disturbed.

faint growl at me feet and looked down to see first one and then two cubs scurrying around in the deep grass. I had somehow slipped between a sow and her two cubs!

I immediately yelled to let her know I was human (and to calm my fears). After all, I reasoned, I was dressed in camo and had my face painted. Maybe she thought I was another bear!

I didn't know it, but the sow had treed. My human voice, however, gave her the courage to come down out of the tree and come at me clicking and popping her jaws. I thought she was going to nail me, and I was terrified! I nocked an arrow and slowly backed away from her and the cubs until I was 20 or 30 yards away. She woofed a few more times, summoning her two cubs to her side. Reunited, the trio fled into the underbrush, leaving me

Black bears can cause extensive damage to hunting camps and equipment left unattended, like canoes and ATV seats.

Black bears often get the rap, but grizzly bears will also break into a camp, as evidenced by the long hairs found on the window ledge.

panting and sweating, but none the worse for the encounter.

TRAIL BOSS

After that episode, I was a little more leery of bow-hunting the tall grass. A few years later, however, I came across another bruin that gave me cause to think about my place in the world. I was still-hunting for deer in New Jersey when I watched a fat bruin pass by only 40 yards distant. It hadn't seen me, and I was thrilled to watch it feed nonchalantly on acorns.

Once it was out of sight, I continued my search for deer when another bruin appeared. This one was going to cross 20 yards in front of me, and it also had no idea I was nearby. I was on a deer trail, so I dropped quietly to one knee to watch the bruin, but when it stepped in front of me, it turned and started walking on the same trail right at me!

I yelled (I do that a lot when I'm scared), and the bear stopped dead in its tracks only to sit down on the trail. Now what was I going to do? I didn't want to give ground, so I picked up a dead log and slammed it into the earth, hoping to scare the bear away. The bruin looked at me hard before slamming its paw down hard on the ground, probably hoping to scare me away. I could feel the ground vibrate!

That's when I noticed the 135-pound bear had both ears filled with metal tags. This bear had been trapped and tagged by state officials, and I couldn't help but wonder why. Was this a problem bear? Had he lost his natural fear of man?

Now I was scared, and I dared not run. I was uphill from the bear, and since it wasn't going to budge, I decided to walk downhill and off the trail, giving it and the high ground to the bruin. It worked. Two minutes later I was standing where the bear had been sitting and the bear was walking up the trail away from me. With a sigh of relief, I turned away, too.

BIG FOOT

Some bears get so good at stealing bait they are almost unkillable. Such was the case in Washington a few years back when Al Miraglia and I went after Big Foot, a black bear so named because of his 6-inch front pads.

This 400-pound bear had the nasty habit of hitting our bait when we weren't in the stand and then stashing as much of the good stuff as possible in the nearby brush. Big Foot could then munch on the bones and honey-soaked bread at his leisure.

One afternoon, Al and I had enough of this bear's

A classic honey burn with sweet smoke drifting into the bush.

does Al's neighbor. He has no idea it is up to him to spook the bear off the bait so I can go home. Frustrated, I whistle to get the driver's attention. The bear is now under my stand, looking up at me. He knows I'm in the tree, and still he stays. Now I'm concerned, as Big Foot is woofing and snarling at me, and my driver is not responding to my whistles.

Finally, I yell at the driver to grab a lantern and come up to the stand. "Why?" he asks me. When I tell him there's a 400-pound bruin under my stand, all he can say is, "Go to Hell!"

Through all the yelling back and forth, Big Foot stayed put, snarling and woofing to beat the band. When the driver finally garnered the courage to approach the stand, Big Foot only stepped back a bit, but it was enough for me to get down. The commotion must have been too much for the bear, however, because he never hit the bait again.

HONEY BEAR

Bears love honey, and boiling a bucket full of the sweet stuff is a great way to attract one to your bait site. One year, however, I got more than I bargained for when a small bear came to the honey burn almost immediately. The bear spotted me in the stand almost as fast, and before I knew it, he was climbing up the tree at me.

I sat perfectly still, thrilled at the prospect of another close encounter, but I became concerned when the bear was on the opposite side of the trunk and only a few inches away from my butt. That's when the bruin started woofing and scaring the pudding out of me. You see, I was hunting alone, and no one knew where I was sitting that night. I was also strapped in and couldn't climb any higher or turn around to save my soul. I realized the bear could easily bite me or claw me, and I wouldn't be able to ward off the blows. I was, as they say, good and stuck.

Then for no apparent reason, the bear became interested in my accessory rope. After licking it for a while, he slid down the tree and walked over to the honey. He looked up at me several times but finally skulked off into the swamp. It's a good thing he was a small bear, because I was shaking too much to draw my bow on a big one.

THE CLIFF BEAR

The bait had been stashed at the base of a cliff about a half-mile from an old logging road, and it was being hit regularly by several bears including one with 5-inch front pads. I took my bow and crawled up the cliff to a small shelf where I had an easy shot straight down at the bait barrel, and I waited. Although I was cornered up there, as there was no exit other than the entrance trail I used to climb the cliff, it seemed like an ideal set-up.

The first time you sit over a bait is often the most exciting, and my first stay on the cliff was no exception. As soon as it settled down, I heard a twig snap behind the bait and then another. A moment later a young boar,

shenanigans. We retrieved all the bait and secured it in such a manner that it would be difficult for Big Foot to drag it off into the woods again.

We waited a couple of nights and then I sat in the treestand. Big Foot was sure to show, and around 6 o'clock, that's exactly what he did. I surmised he was not happy about his missing food stash, and he let me know by snarling and pacing back and forth. He would not, however, step into bow range. Darkness finally came, but the bear stayed in the brush woofing and snarling.

Now, Al and I have a standing agreement that if one of us is not at the pick-up point, the other will grab a light and come looking. More often than not, a bear has one of us treed. The light usually scares the bear away, and the integrity of the stand is saved. Well that night we had Al's neighbor as a driver, and he knew nothing about our unwritten rule.

As I sat in my stand, Big Foot circled the bait, waiting for complete darkness before committing himself to the set-up. In the meantime, I'm caught up in the tree. If I lower myself to the ground, the bear will know our plan and avoid the site altogether. Of course, no one wants to meet a bear in the dark on the exit path, either.

Al's neighbor finally drives the truck to within 75 yards of the treestand, but the bear stays put and so probably 125-pounds, emerged from the undergrowth and began feeding on the discarded bones and meat scraps.

All of a sudden, he looked straight up at me, his beady little eyes burning holes through me like laser beams, and began popping his jaws. He was obviously angry over something; maybe he thought I was another bear. Whatever was going through his head, the young boar clawed his way up a nearby tree for a better look at me before sliding back down to the ground.

What happened next left my palms sweaty for days. The young boar, "woofing" in a staccato-like fashion, charged up the cliff at me, stopping only a few yards from my crouched position, and began swaying his head back and forth in front of me.

I picked up a small stick to defend myself, as if that would help, turned sideways and averted my eyes from those of the bear. I hoped my body language and look of deference would have a positive effect on the bruin's attitude. It actually seemed to work, too, for the bear soon stopped hissing and slid back a few yards.

Then, inexplicably, the young boar lunged at me with paws outstretched, stopping this time only a few feet away. I was sure now he was going to bite me, or worse, but then he backed down the cliff a few yards.

A few minutes passed and I thought his antics were over, but they were not. He lowered his face, saliva dripping to the ground, and began inching his way towards me, one outstretched paw after the other, like he was stalking his next meal.

I held my ground, gripping my club with determination while fearing all the while he would lunge if I moved one inch. I wasn't about to become bowhunter burger, yet I only had a head shot, which is really no shot at all.

Just then, a twig snapped behind the bait. The young boar quickly took notice, and much to my relief, he disappeared down the cliff and into the brush. What scared him away? A 300-pound sow with five—that's right—five cubs coming into the bait! After my encounter with the young boar, I decided retreat was the better part of valor, and I vacated the cliff bait but not before avowing never to sit on the ground next to a bait pile again without a gun—and a big gun at that—for back-up. It is just too risky otherwise.

As you can see, bear hunting can have its exciting moments. It's hard to believe how big a bear can get until you see one up close and personal. Nonetheless, black bear attacks are few and far between; they are generally more afraid of you than you are of them.

Since man's first encounter with them, black bears have been immortalized.

Classic Bear Hunts

A good bear hunt is often the hunt of a lifetime. Here are three great hunts!

THE HIP POCKET BEAR
Some bears are just born mean.

It's a fact. Some black bears are more dangerous than other black bears. Normally a bruin will avoid all contact with human beings, electing to skulk about in the shadows rather than risk an encounter. In this sense, they are elusive and quite difficult to see in the wild.

But every so often a bear steps out of the bush with an attitude, and the body weight to back it up. These bears can be extremely aggressive and will charge a human being without apparent provocation. These are the bears we read about, the bears that maul and sometimes kill hikers and berry pickers. I ran into such a bear in the fall of 1998 while bowhunting with Bob Heyde's Homestead Outfitters in central Alberta. It was a hair-raising encounter.

I was bowhunting the early season with five permits in my hip pocket: whitetail, mule deer, antlered moose and two black bear tags. Since I was booked for a month, I felt my chances of filling a bear tag and either a moose or deer tag were reasonably good. Actually, I figured the bear would be a piece of cake. I had hunted with Homestead Outfitters several times in the past, and each trip resulted in at least one opportunity at a trophy-sized 300-plus-pound bruin. As it turned out, this trip would be no exception.

There was just one twist, however. I didn't want to take another black bear over bait. Instead, I wanted to arrow a black bear from the ground, and the place to do this is the farm country 5 hours north of Edmonton where black bears are known to ravage oat fields with abandon. Bears here feed almost like whitetails. That is, they bed in woodlots during the day and then sneak out into the fields of standing oats to feed in the evening. The trick would be to catch one en route to the field, or slip up onto one as he gorged himself along the perimeter of the field. The shooting could be, as they say, up close and personal.

I had an opportunity at a bear my first evening afield. A 300-pound jumbo walked brazenly out of the bush a mere 35 yards in front of me before continuing across an open alfalfa lot without ever looking back. The distance, however, was simply too great for me to try a shot with my recurve. I frantically tried to close the distance, but the bear soon melted into the bush on the far side of the field. I never saw him again.

The next evening our host, David Marx, showed me one of his oat fields that was constantly being raided by black bears. Within minutes, we caught a fat bear parked about 40 yards from the bush sweeping oats into his mouth without a care in the world. It looked like a "gimme," so I grabbed my bow and started stalking the chocolate-colored bear. The wind changed, however, and immediately alerted the bruin to my presence. This bear soon melted into the bush, too.

The next morning David's wife, Paulette, told us a huge black bear had chased a neighbor across an oat field. This farmer, who up to then had no fear of bears, was quite stunned by the incident. Apparently, he had exited his pickup to shoo a bruin away from a grain truck that was left in the field overnight. But instead of running, the bear, snarling and woofing loudly, held his ground.

Realizing he was dealing with an aggressive and potentially dangerous bear, the farmer decided to leave well enough alone, turned his back on the bruin, and started walking towards his pickup. That's when the bear charged. The farmer, running now, reached the safety of his pickup in time, but was mortified when the big blackie attacked his truck instead, smashing his paws into the door, rear-view mirror and front fender. The incident took place in an oat field adjacent to the one we had hunted the previous evening. Little did I know then that I, too, would have a life-threatening encounter with that 375-pound boar.

Now, a big black bear boar is nothing to fool around

Terrain features that promote bear travel such as gentle slopes that lead in and out of swamps are good places to catch a bear.

with. Despite his apparent clumsiness and sometimes clown-like antics, he is a predator at the top of his food chain. He is heavily boned and well muscled, and he likes to fight, as evidenced by the deep scars many old bears carry. His canine teeth are big, and his claws can rip a 4-foot log apart with ease. Indeed, black bears have been known to kill cows, pigs, sheep, horses, dogs and, on occasion, bull moose with little fanfare.

A human being in this regard is simply no match for an enraged black bear. He can easily outrun you, and contrary to what you may have seen on television or in the circus, a black bear can outmaneuver any World Champion professional wrestler.

You are not safe in a treestand either. A black bear can climb 20 feet up a tree faster than you can read this sentence. And if that isn't enough, a mature boar is nearly twice the size of a grown man, averaging 250 pounds in the fall, with 500-pound specimens common enough. Indeed, I've tagged several bears over the years with archery tackle that tipped the scales at 400 pounds or more. But none of these bears were aggressive.

I've had several close encounters with other black bears that scared the pudding out of me, however. I've had bears pad by my head at night while I rested comfortably inside a canvas tent. I've had bears follow me back to my truck in the dark, clacking their teeth only yards

Some bears are born mean. Here's the author with the Hip Pocket Bear.

In wilderness areas, any beaver caught on land or in shallow water is doomed. Bears love beavers almost as much as they do honey.

behind me. I've had bears stalk within 10 yards of me while a pal wailed on an elk-calf call. I've sat on the ground within yards of a bait site and photographed groups of bears as they fed greedily nearby. I've had bears charge me at a bait site only to run like hell when I stood up yelling and waving my arms. I've also had bears stand their ground, forcing me to back away and walk around them. I've had bears woof at me from the base of the tree, keeping me in my stand until help arrived. I've had other bruins actually climb up and try to get into the treestand with me. I even walked between a sow and two cubs one day while still-hunting for deer, almost stepping on the cute little tykes, and had momma bear quite upset with me—but she did not attack me. The Hip Pocket Bear, however, was different. He did not fear humans—he despised them.

THE HUNT

The evening started off easy enough. While searching the edge of a large oat field for activity, I glassed a large bear a quarter mile away just emerging from the bush to feed in the oats. I tried to put the sneak on that bruin, but he soon disappeared into the bush. Heyde, who had been walking behind me with a 30-30, thought I was going too fast and had walked right past the bear. I turned around, and sure enough, there was indeed a bear moving through the bush about 30 yards from the edge of the field, but it was just too thick to risk a shot. That bruin was soon swallowed up by the shadows. We both thought it was the bear I had been stalking, and since he had seen us, the hunt was over for the evening. We didn't realize several bears were feeding regularly in this field.

We decided to split up then and scout our way back to the parked Dodge. It seemed like a good idea at the time. The thought of running into a nasty bear now was the last thing on our minds. I wasn't gone 10 minutes, however, when I stumbled upon a concentration of black bear sign along the edge of an uncut oat field. Large diameter droppings and well-worn trails littered with tracks from 5-inch front pads told me a huge boar was spending a lot of time in the immediate vicinity.

I slipped into the bush and slowly started to still-hunt through the thick stuff. There was bear sign everywhere, giving my adrenal glands a hefty workout. The adrenaline really started flowing 20 minutes later though when I caught a large bruin off guard, sitting on his haunches and yawning like a junkyard dog only 40 yards distant. The range and thick cover made a bow shot impossible, so I decided to ease forward when the bear got up on all fours, put his nose to the ground and started walking in my general direction.

I tried to find a hole in the brush to shoot through, but there was none to be had. Suddenly, the bear sensed something was wrong, turned his head and looked right at me. He wasted no time. Standing up on his hind legs,

One of the secrets to fall baiting is to set up shop in an area where bears are already congregating, such as this oat field, which was trampled by hungry bruins.

he began to hiss loudly. When he turned slightly sideways to me, dropped to all fours and laid his ears back, I knew I was in trouble. Without further warning, the big bear raised his 5-inch front pads off the ground a foot or so, and after emitting a series of "woofs" in staccato-like fashion, charged.

I never had a chance to come to full draw. Dead branches were snapped in two like matchsticks as the enraged bear lunged forward, stopping less than 30 feet from me. He stood up on his hind legs again, raked a 6-inch aspen with his claws and began pushing back and forth on the trunk like he was trying to uproot the whole tree.

If he was trying to scare me, it worked. The bear was enormous, nearly twice my size, with beady little eyes, no neck and massive front legs. He dropped back down to all fours and just stared at me head-on hissing loudly. Slowly, the 375-pound boar backed up a bit and started pacing back and forth in front of me, never taking his eyes off me. I came to full draw on two occasions, but again could not find an opening in the brush to shoot. The boar stopped pacing and sat on his haunches just staring at me for what seemed like forever before turning to slowly walk away from me.

That's when I made a foolish mistake. I took a few steps in his direction looking for a clear path for my arrow. The bear, apparently enraged by my forward movement, pivoted on his front feet and charged me again. This time I thought I was going to be badly bitten.

The bear seemed to be on a mission, his staccato-like woofs even louder than before. I held my ground, hoping for an opportunity to drill him with an arrow, and knowing full well there was no use running. The boar suddenly stopped in the same place as last time and again stood up to maul the aspen, hissing all the while.

The big blackie then dropped to all fours and turned to walk away, but changing his mind in mid-stride, he swung his head about to sit down on his haunches so he could stare at me some more. I dared

Body weight and skull size are not the only criterion used to distinguish one bear from another. Color-phase bears like this cinnamon bear are much sought after trophies.

not move this time.

A few minutes later the bear got up and waddled slowly back into the bush. I got on a bear trail and quickly closed the distance between us. When he passed in front of me, he must have caught me moving out of the corner of his eye. He spun around in my direction for a better look-see, but when he did, he gave me a clear 15-yard broadside shot. I immediately brought my Mathews Conquest to full draw, aimed and sent a TNT-tipped 2514 in his direction. The shaft passed completely through the bear, leaving plenty of red blood at the wound sight.

Roaring loudly, the huge bear bit at the arrow wound several times before climbing 10 feet into a nearby 16-inch aspen. Instinct took over then I guess, because for some reason, I charged the bear, sending him another 15 feet up the tree.

I was elated when I reached the base of the aspen and gazed skyward at the huge boar, but the elation lasted only a few short seconds. That's when he looked down at me, and without any hesitation, started inching his way out of the tree. I was horrified. There was no way I was going to let this bear get to ground zero, but I couldn't find a clear opening through all the leafy branches to shoot. I finally got right underneath him and tried to send a second shaft from his tail to his chest. I didn't get the penetration I wanted, but it did push the bear to the very top of the aspen.

I could hear blood dripping onto the ground now, but I wasn't taking any chances. I stepped back away from the tree, nocked another shaft and shot once more. This time the broadhead angled deep into his chest. The bear teetered a bit at the top for a few seconds, and then fell 40 feet like a baby grand piano, breaking branches off—some the size of my leg—all the way down. The bear hit the ground with a resounding THUD, and then unbelievably, he uprighted himself, spun around and charged.

This time I ran, quickly, just knowing the bear was going to sink his teeth into me. I somehow managed to get behind a large aspen, pulled my last arrow from my quiver and turned to face the bear. I was astonished to find him standing only a few feet away, swinging his great head back and forth like a crazed drug addict waving a gun in my face!

We stood eyeball-to-eyeball for several seconds before I realized the fight was out of him. He slowly turned his back to me and after zigzagging 50 yards or so through the bush, expired without further incident.

We got the bear back to the ranch, and due to the 70-degree temperature, decided to skin him out that evening. There wasn't nearly as much fat on the bear as I would have expected for this time of the year. The poor berry crop may have been one of the reasons for his aggressive disposition.

If I had to do it over again, I don't know if I would do anything differently. Looking back, the whole incident from the time I saw the bear sitting on his haunches to the time he came crashing out of the tree was probably only 4 or 5 minutes. It was, however, a very long 4 or 5 minutes—minutes I know I will never forget.

ALBERTA'S TROPHY BLACK BEARS

Big bears don't come easy!

"Look at the size of that bear!" I yelled as the 4X4 rocked & rolled along the old farm road. "It's as big as a Volkswagen!"

"Your crazy, Vaznis," stammered Eric as he slammed on the breaks. "That's no bear, it's a runaway cow!"

I handed Eric my Zeiss glasses as soon as the Powerwagon screeched to a halt, but he didn't really need them. Instinct had already told him that the large dark object waddling some 1000 yards in the distance was indeed a huge black bear.

"He's magnificent," whispered Eric, as if the big bruin could actually hear us. "Look at him strut his stuff!"

And strut that bear did. We spent the next few minutes watching that bruin swing his wide head back and

Rifle hunters can sit aloft overlooking ripe farm crops, but bowhunters need to be back in the bush where close shots are more likely.

forth as he methodically worked his way along the far edge of a cut oat field. Eventually, the over-450-pound boar crossed the yellow stubble field and then disappeared into a sea of uncut grain less than 100 yards from my treestand.

"Is he big enough for you?" asked Eric with a broad grin on his face.

"Big enough!" I replied. "He's a once-in-a-lifetime bear. Let's go get him."

"Well, it looks like he already beat us to the bait. We can hurry on to another treestand, or you can try and catch him on the bait right now. What do you want to do?"

What did I want to do? What a question! Of course I wanted a crack at that big bear. As it turned out, I spent all but one of the next 8 days trying to catch "Volkswagen" at that bait.

Eric Grinnell with the author's "Volkswagen" bear.

TROPHY BEARS

Deer hunters have long known that Alberta is home to some prodigious whitetail bucks. What many people don't know, however, is that the province also has a healthy population of oversized black bears. According to John Gunson, large carnivore manager for the province of Alberta, the province is crawling with bears.

"There are two reasons why we have a good population of black bears," says Gunson. "One is habitat. Unlike some other provinces, our soils support an aspen-dominated forest that produces a wide variety of nutritious bear foods.

"Secondly, resident and non-resident hunting pressure has, until recently, been quite low. This means that in many areas bears are either lightly hunted or not hunted at all. This limited fascination with bears and bear hunting has left a high number of older, mature males in the population."

Interest in harvesting record-book bears has been on the rise, however, with Alberta outfitters now accessing many of those once wilderness regions. As a consequence, Gunson and other researchers have developed a more intensive bear management program for the province. Alberta now enforces an allocation system that equitably divides the resource between residents and non-residents. Hopefully, this will ensure a combined harvest not in excess of provincial guidelines and a future supply of trophy black bears for many generations to come.

How big are Alberta's black bears? Well, they are not any bigger than black bears found elsewhere across North America; it's just that the average black bear living in Alberta is an older, more mature specimen. For example, in a good year, 35 to 40 percent of the spring harvest will weigh between 200 and 450 pounds. Indeed, spring bears in excess of 400 pounds are not at all uncommon, and many fall bears weighing 600 or more pounds have been recorded. Since the word is just now getting out, only a few of these big bruisers are listed in any of the record books. Nonetheless, outfitters like Eric Grinnell report at least 20 percent of their annual spring take qualifies for the Pope & Young club.

Body weight and skull size are not the only criteria used to compare one bear to another. For many people, including myself, the color and condition of the hide must also be taken into consideration. Alberta, like a number of other western states and provinces, has a fair number of color-phase black bears. Cinnamon, chocolate brown, red, and blond can often be found in pockets scattered throughout the province. In fact, what initially brought me to Alberta was the possibility of not only tagging a heavy, mature blackie, but maybe a color-phase boar as well.

FALL HUNTING TECHNIQUES

Spring bears are finicky eaters, dining primarily on the earliest of greenery. They will, of course, take advantage of any winter-killed carrion they stumble upon, and on occasion, they may even kill a fawn or calf. Nonetheless, their average caloric input during this period barely meets their daily nutritional requirements. Manmade bait piles become a welcome food source then, and black bears will visit these stashes regularly if given the opportunity. In fact, where legal, hunting over bait is the preferred method for collecting a springtime version of *Ursus americanus*.

Baiting, however, has not been as successful in the fall primarily because a cornucopia of natural foods exists for the bears, and manhandled goodies just can't compete with such a bounty. After all, why would a 500-pound boar come to a 10-pound pile of beef scraps and candy bars when he has a whole ridge full of high-calorie beechnuts to feed on?

Well, at least up until now, that has been the conventional wisdom. That is, fall baiting just doesn't work as well. But what would happen if a bait station was situated near a known fall food source, such as cultivated oats, instead of along some far away beaver dam? Would the bruins ignore the offering, or "hit" the bait on their way to those preferred feeding areas?

"The reason Grinnell and Silvertip Outfitters has been so successful with their fall baiting operation," says Gunson, "is that they are baiting near food sources already being heavily utilized by concentrations of fall bears. Under these circumstances, no bear can refuse a free meal."

Indeed, farmers I spoke with reported seeing up to 22 bears in a single grain field. They welcomed hunters and often helped outfitters locate preferred feeding areas prior to the season opener. In fact, they were so helpful, I passed up 11 black bears during my stay.

THE HUNT

I went right after "Volkswagen" the first evening we spotted him, but he was nowhere to be found. He wasn't around the next evening either. The oat field was being harvested on the third day, so I hurried over to Ernie Weinrich's Spotted Horse Lake Farm some 10 miles away and climbed into another treestand. It was a good move. An hour before dark, I watched in awe as a huge cinnamon boar cautiously approached my position. He sniffed about the bait pile for a second or two before sneaking off with a large chunk of meat in his mouth.

I thought I might have blown the shot, but the big boar returned 20 minutes later. This time he lingered long enough at the bait to present me with a classic broadside shot. The razor-tipped camo shaft easily sliced through both lungs causing the 300-pound bruin to expire in less than 10 seconds.

If my hunt had ended right then and there, I would have been satisfied. After all, the thick underfur and vibrant color of this Alberta bear were a dream come true. Nonetheless, I still had a second tag, and "Volkswagen" still roamed nearby.

On the last day of my scheduled hunt, a huge black bear padded into the bait right before dark. I pulled my Jennings Carbon Extreme back to full draw twice, but the big blackie failed to give me a clean-kill shot, so I passed. I'm sure now that big bear was "Volkswagen."

My hunt was officially over, but the next morning Grinnell took a few minutes and studied my plane reservations. "You know Bill," said Eric with a smile on his face, "if Air Canada will let you fly out of Edmonton tomorrow afternoon instead of Dawson Creek this evening, you can have one more chance at 'Volkswagen.'"

I telephoned the airport immediately and then unpacked. Later that evening, I sat near the oat field one last time.

Another day was about to come to an end as the sun, once a bright orange disk high in the sky, slid slowly down behind the trees. There was a stirring then, no more than a whisper really, somewhere deep in the swamp. At first it seemed like a ruffed grouse faintly drumming on a far away log, or a coyote searching the tall grass for a mouse or two. It was neither, for suddenly an enormous creature stepped into view and tested the wind with huge, flaring nostrils. He stood there for a full minute weaving his great head back and forth until he was satisfied all was clear. Then without further hesitation, the beast left the cover of the swamp and padded towards a cache of carrion some 300 yards in the distance.

He had been there many times before and had always fed greedily on the discarded bones and meat. Tonight would be no exception as the boar worked his way through the mixed spruce-fir and willow tangles that separated the swamp from a field of harvested grain—and his last meal.

"Volkswagen" had always been cautious near this bait. Maybe it was the scent of man that alerted him; maybe it was the odor of other bears. Whatever it was, the big bruin decided to wait a few minutes downwind from the cache before committing himself to feed. Only after he was sure the area was unattended did he leave the safety of the shadows and step cautiously into the failing light.

I was glad I hadn't risked a shot the evening before because the P&Y bear was much more relaxed on this evening. He was so intent on chowing down, in fact, he never saw me bring my 70# Jennings Carbon Extreme to full draw, hold and then release a razor-tipped 2115 camo shaft towards his vitals.

The arrow struck with a resounding whack, passed completely through the bear and then lodged in the ground beyond. Surprisingly, "Volkswagen" did not bolt but instead turned and walked slowly back towards the safety of the swamp. He coughed once en route and then laid down for the last time 50 yards from the treestand.

BIG SKY BRUINS
Tagging a fall bear is one-third luck and two-thirds guile.

At first I thought I was dreaming. But then the glare from a 60-watt bulb and the soft putt-putt-putt of a distant generator told me I was once more in bear camp, this time tucked away somewhere along the Yaak in northwestern Montana.

It took me a few seconds to gather my senses, but eventually I unzipped my sleeping bag and swung my feet out onto the warm floor of the tent. I quickly dressed and stepped outside into the cold air to wash my face and brush my teeth. The September sky was full of bright stars, ten hundred thousand maybe, shining down at me like they can nowhere else in the world. This was definitely Big Sky country, and I took a few moments to appreciate the spectacle.

Back in the tent, Steve, Bruce, Tony and Mike were all getting themselves ready for breakfast. We gathered in the cook tent a few minutes later where we all wolfed down bacon and eggs and a gallon or so of black coffee—much to Maria's delight. We made our own bag lunches and then "moseyed" on down to the coral where Timmy and the boys were busy arranging gear and saddling the horses.

"Let's get a move on," barked Tim over the putt-putt-putt of the generator. "It's getting late, and we need to be

Lunch in the high country. Keep a sharp eye because a boar can materialize any time of the day.

on top of the mountain before first light."

Saddlebags were stuffed with lunches, rain gear and other essentials. Gary and young Tony double-checked the saddles one more time before each of us swung our legs up and over.

"Everybody set?" asked Tim from somewhere in the darkness. "Steve, you get behind me and Chief. Tony, you and Mike follow Steve. Jeff, check on their stirrups and then you and Bruce follow Mike. Now keep an eye on those horses when we get near the creek. They'll want to stop and bunch up, but keep 'em moving. Jon, you go last and make sure Vaznis doesn't fall off Red Cloud again! Let's go!"

For the next half-hour or so, we rode silently through the brush and deep grass before starting up the mountain. We crossed the trickle of a creek without incident and headed into the black timber where only the sparks from the horses' hooves lit the trail. Ducking branches, we zigzagged through a steep switchback before resting in a little hollow at the base of the "elevator."

"Wait your turn and don't crowd," said Tim after everyone got re-acquainted. "When you're ready, just lean forward and give 'em the lead. And hang on!"

Soon, Chief, Red Cloud and the rest of the string were lunging straight up the "elevator" amidst a mixture of dust, creaking leather and loud whinnies. Somehow, we all made it up to the upper rim without

falling or slipping off into the darkness.

We stopped at the top to gather our forces and then watched in awe as Mt. Kento appeared mysteriously off in the distance, its treeless peak lit only by the first rays of the early morning sun. We were all searching for bears now, and although we didn't see any just then, each of us somehow knew we would all get a crack at a trophy bruin sometime during the upcoming week.

MONTANA BEAR FACTS

To many eastern hunters, Montana conjures up images of bugling elk and hat-racked mulies, but we were after *Ursus americanus*, the North American black bear. Now, there's nothing wrong with hunting either of those two ungulates, but black bears have always been a fascination for me, as they are for thousands of other sportsman scattered across the continent.

According to Vince Yannone, avid bear hunter and assistant administrator for the state's Conservation Education Division, a Big Sky bruin can be found almost anywhere in the state, with the northwest corner getting the nod as one of THE places to go for a big bruin.

"Nobody knows for sure how many black bears there are in Montana," says Yannone, "but the annual harvest is around 800. Our fall boars usually weigh in the neighborhood of 225 pounds, which is a good bear anywhere. Sows on the same range are generally 45 to 50 pounds less."

A horse and a flat-shooting rifle, what more can a bear hunter ask for?

Keep in mind these are averages, and the average Montana bruin is tagged near good access. If you want a better-than-average black bear, you must go high up in the mountains where the hunting pressure is light, and the bears roam undisturbed. Indeed, anything under 200 pounds is often considered to be quite small for a horse-back hunt in the Rockies!

Larger bears aren't the only reason to climb into a saddle. Many hunters want their trophy-sized bruin to be off-color, too. About one-half of Montana's bears are jet black, but the remainder vary from chocolate brown to red, cinnamon or blond—a rarity anywhere "back east." Some bears even sport a multi-colored pelage!

One of the most beautiful black bears I have ever seen was a color-phase specimen. Jon spotted the blond and cinnamon boar feeding in an open meadow back in 1988. We watched the bear for some time before I attempted a stalk, but, unfortunately, the big bear eluded me before I could get off a shot. I can still see his blond shoulders and cinnamon-colored back shimmering in the early morning light as he fed on fat huckleberries along the south slope of Mt. Kento. He was a sight to behold!

Sometimes the "trophy" qualities of a black bear, however, have nothing to do with hide color or body size—it's the way the bear was tagged that separates one bruin from another! Since baiting and dogs are both illegal in Montana, we hoped to first spot a bruin from above and then sneak to within shooting distance. I wanted to bow-

bag my bruin, while others in the party were relying on their skills with a rifle to put a rug on the wall. By week's end, we all had our chances at that bear of a lifetime, and although I did indeed get a bruin in the end, it didn't quite work out the way any of us had planned.

FALL BRUINS—THE SECRET TO SUCCESS

Most black bears tagged in the fall are taken by hunters in search of other game. In the East, the bulk of the bear harvest takes place during the regular big-game season when deer hunters and bruins so often blunder into each other.

Taking a fall bear by design, however, requires more than mere luck; it takes lots of hard work and planning. As mentioned in an earlier chapter, come autumn, bears enter a stage called hyperphagia, or excessive eating, where they range far and wide in search of caloric-rich forage. They strive to store enough fat at this time to sustain themselves during the upcoming denning period.

On good range, a fall bruin can actually increase his body weight 2.2 or more pounds a day! Fall bears will often congregate near oak hollows, beech ridges, apple orchards, cultivated grain fields and berry patches. If you can manage to concentrate your hunting efforts near a proven fall food source, your chances of collecting a trophy size bear are very good indeed.

THE PLAN

In northwestern Montana, the huckleberry crop attracts lots of bears, especially if there is plentiful rain and warm temperatures during the growing season.

"If we are fortunate, these berries start ripening in the lower elevations around the first of June," says Tim. "Then as they dry and drop to the ground, others ripen at progressively higher elevations until only the upper basins have sweet berries when the fall hunting season arrives.

"The plan then is to first get on top of the mountain and methodically glass the various basins and open slopes for feeding bears. First light and dusk are the best times to be afield, but a good bear can be spotted at almost any time of the day.

"We know, too, from experience that bears will keep coming back to a patch of berries as long as the food lasts. We, therefore, will sometimes sit above a berry-laden basin all day if need be until a bear steps out into the open to feed."

That's exactly what happened one late afternoon as Jon and I glassed a likely looking basin 3 or 4 hours from camp. We knew the meadow held ripe berries because another member of our party had glassed a nice bear there earlier in the week. Sure enough, after a long vigil we spotted a six-and-a-half-footer working his way through the tall timber and towards the open meadow to feed. Once Jon confirmed the bear's size, I used my Zeiss 8X30B's to help plan an approach path.

It was a difficult stalk—almost impossible really—so Jon politely offered me the use of his bolt-action rifle. I was tempted, but I wanted to tag the bear with my bow and arrow, so I pressed forward. I should have listened to Jon because before I could get close enough for a shot with my Carbon Extreme, the bear meandered into a nearby drainage never to be seen again. This was the second time in as many trips that I had passed on the use of Jon's scoped 30-06 in favor of the bow, and it was the second time the bear disappeared into the underbrush unscathed. I vowed that wouldn't happen again on this trip.

TROPHY BRUINS

By this time, everybody in camp had seen some whopper bruins, but it took the crack shooting of two Texas lawmen to bring the first bears to bag. Mike Hamilton took a fine 300 pounder from 225 yards with his 300 Weatherby Magnum. One shot through the junction of the bruin's head and neck with a factory 180-grain Nosler Partition put his six-and-a-half-footer down for keeps. This was Mike's first bear, and it was a dandy!

The biggest bear of all, however, was tagged by Tony Black, a veteran of the Dallas Police Department. Tony's on the SWAT team, and he was able to put his honed shooting skills to good use in the mountains. Here's what happened.

One afternoon, Tony and Tim spotted a large chocolate and blond bear working its way through the alders near the edge of a steep basin. When the bruin raised its head, both Tim and Tony thought it was a black bear, but the hump on the bruin's back and the two-toned coloration made them both want to double-check before shooting. Grizzly bears are fully protected in Montana.

"By now," said Tony, "the bear was 325 yards away and positioned downhill at a 45-degree angle. Only when the bear raised its head again were we both sure it was not a grizzly. The first shot from my 300 Weatherby Magnum hit the shoulder and passed completely through the bear's chest. The bear rolled immediately over on his back and stuck both feet straight up in the air, but Tim yelled 'shoot again!' so I did, putting another 180-grain Nosler Partition through the bear's chest. My third shot hit the bear in the head and neck as it rolled end-over-end down the mountain. That handload easily traveled through the bear's chest and diaphragm and exited on the opposite side of the body."

Tony and Tim estimated the live weight of the trophy boar to be between 450 and 500 pounds. In fact, they needed help just to roll the bruin over for skinning! Back at camp, a steel tape revealed measurements of 7' 7" paw-to-paw, and 6' 8" nose-to-tail, making it truly the bear of a lifetime.

TOO MANY BEARS

On the last day of my hunt, Jon, Tony and I spotted a large bruin feeding unconcerned along a far-away slope. After deciding he was indeed a keeper, we rode the horses a mile back around the top of Mt. Kento so we could sneak up on the six-and-a-half-footer from above and with the wind in our favor.

It took us a while to spot the boar once we arrived on the upper rim. In fact, we thought the bear had simply disappeared, like so many of them tend to do, when Jon suddenly spotted it feeding a hundred yards or so away from where we had last seen it. Unfortunately, the bear was now almost 300 yards directly below our position where loose rocks and thick brush made a stalk impossible.

I was disappointed, but Tony again offered me the use of his scoped 300 Weatherby Magnum. After thinking about what happened on two earlier occasions, I laid down my Carbon Extreme and readied myself for a difficult rifle shot. This was no time to be a purist!

For half an hour, we watched the bruin weave in and out of the shadows. At one point, he walked through a small opening in the brush, offering me a perfect broadside shot. We could then see it was indeed a beautiful chocolate brown specimen—not jet black as we one time thought—but my unfamiliarity with the Kahle's picketpost reticle cost me the shot. By the time I had his vitals picked out in the scope, the bear had again disappeared.

I changed shooting positions five times in the next 10 minutes in an effort to keep the bear in view. Time and time again we would spot a piece of the bear in the underbrush, but we could never see quite enough hide for a clean one-shot kill. Frankly, I was getting dizzy looking down into the canyon, and I doubt I would have tried the shot had Tony not been there coaching me.

Finally, the bruin looked as if he were about to pass through another small opening, so I hunkered down behind the scope. I listened to Tony one more time, and when the bruin stepped clear, I settled the scope and squeezed the trigger.

The shot felt good, and after the echoes faded, Tony lowered himself into the canyon for a look-see while Jon and I stayed on top in case the bruin broke from cover.

There was no need for concern, however, as the bullet hit its intended mark behind the shoulder, killing the bear almost instantly.

We were all stunned, though, when we finally walked up on the downed animal. It was not the chocolate six-and-a-half-footer we had been watching, but a coal-black yearling with huckleberry stains all over his face. Unbeknownst to us, there were at least two bears in the basin that morning, and I had unfortunately shot the smaller of the two.

Nonetheless, I tagged the young boar, whose weight was generously estimated to be around 100 pounds, and brought him back to camp. It certainly was not the bear Jon, Tim or myself had in mind, but he was a legal bear taken fair and square, and I was proud of him and the steep 300-yard shot it took to get him. I guess in some respects that makes him the bear of a lifetime, too.

From a distance, the tan shoulders on this black bear looked like a hump, one of the distinguishing characteristics of a grizzly bear.

Mistakes to Avoid

Patience is often the key to success when hunting black bears!

Somehow I knew this was the spot. We were hunting deep in the Manitoba wilderness some 2 or 3 hours north of Flin Flon in an area noted for large, color-phase black bears. Our bait had been placed just off an abandoned logging road that bisected a large lake into two tea-stained ponds ringed with clumps of tall grass and 8-foot-high alders. A variety of wildlife had been using the old road to get from one side of the lake to the other, including a pack of wolves and a couple of good sized black bears that found the pastries and meat scraps much to their liking. By the end of the week, attorney Marshall Whalley and I would each tag a beautiful chocolate-phase bruin from this site.

Outfitters Jack Smith and Glen Whitbread had erected a treestand 15 feet from the ground and 15 yards from the bait in a lone spruce tree that overlooked the offering before leaving the area to cool down for a couple of days. One afternoon when the wind was in my favor, I sneaked down the grown-over logging road and eased myself up into that stand for an evening of fall bear hunting.

I didn't have long to wait. I heard a branch crack in the brush behind the bait about 90 minutes before dark and then a few moments later another twig snapped. Suddenly, a trophy-colored bruin was milling around the site sampling a little bit of this and a little bit of that before finally settling in on some beef scraps he found laying in the bottom of a large metal barrel. As soon as he stuck his head inside the drum for a second helping, I brought my bow to full draw and released a full-length Easton XX75 camo shaft at his vitals. The 2514 tipped with a 100-grain Satellite Titan did the job, and the bruin perished on the run a few seconds after the shot.

That was my third bruin that season, and I was excited in part because the bear hunt had gone as planned. We had a good camp with good guides, good food and good companionship. It was, to say the least, a good time, but not all hunts have such happy endings. All it takes is one slip-up to ruin an otherwise terrific adventure. In this chapter we will discuss some of the most common mistakes that bear hunters make; mistakes you'll want to avoid on your next bear hunt.

Jeff Grab, of NorthCountry Expeditions, gets hundreds of requests for black bear hunts each year. According to him, the biggest mistake a bow, muzzleloader or rifle hunter can make is to book a bear trip with an unqualified outfitter.

"If you are serious about taking a black bear," says Grab, "then you must book with an outfitter that takes his bear hunting seriously. Sure, you can always find a guy who will throw some dead fish behind your cabin for you, but your chances of seeing a trophy bear under these conditions are usually quite slim.

"What you want is an outfitter who is willing to work hard for you and one who has a 'graduate degree' in black bear behavior. In short, you need a pro who has a proven track record of regularly producing quality bears for his clients."

Grab's advice should be etched into your brain. Over the years I have been fortunate enough to hunt bears with some of the best outfitters in North America. Each enjoys plenty of repeat business in part because they help their clients avoid certain pitfalls. Here is what they recommend.

Brian MacVicar of Atlantic Adventures in New Brunswick urges his clients "to be as familiar with their weapon as possible before coming to camp. There is nothing more heart breaking for a hunter than to blow an easy shot at a record-book bear simply because he wasn't prepared. For example, if you are hunting over bait, rifle hunters should be sighted in to hit dead on at 75 yards, not 300! You don't want to have to guess where to aim when you have a fat bruin peering at you from behind a nearby log. And leave that big magnum home! More bears have been killed with a 30-30 than a 458. Besides, you are more likely to flinch with a big bore than something in

Full camouflage helps disguise those involuntary movements we all seem to make on stand.

Good outfitters understand bear behavior, interpret bear behavior correctly and work hard to get you a shot. Why would you hunt with anybody else?

the 270 to 30-06 class. Finally, fire a few rounds soon after you arrive in camp. Airlines and 4x4's have a nasty habit of knocking gun sights out of whack.

"Muzzleloaders have their own set of problems," adds MacVicar, "especially sidelocks and flintlocks. A couple strips of electrician's tape over the muzzle and an extra shot of dry powder inside the nipple will help insure a clean burn even under the wettest of conditions. Nonetheless, blackpowder enthusiasts should get into the habit of shooting and reloading every day before going on stand. To rely on a two-day old charge only increases your chances of a misfire.

"And as for bowhunters, they should only shoot a bow they are comfortable with. They don't need to up the poundage on their whitetail set-up just to arrow a bruin. Sixty pounds is plenty! However, their bow should be well tuned so it launches a quiet, wobble-free shaft. They should also practice from a treestand with a head net in place before the actual hunt. More than one bruin has escaped unscathed because a bowhunter failed to take that bulky netting into account. And for those bowmen who shoot with a release, I suggest they stow a spare in their fanny pack. The last thing they want to have to do is slip out of their stand in the near dark to fetch a release they inadvertently dropped to the ground."

Jack Smith, a former Adirondack bear guide who has set up shop in Manitoba, believes his clients would be more successful if they better understood black bears. "The ability to correctly interpret bear behavior as a hunt-

ing situation unfolds often spells the difference between tagging an average specimen and a record-book animal," says Smith. "Here is a common scenario. Let's say you are hunting a stand where a very big bear has been sighted on a couple of occasions. Suddenly, a nice bear appears in front of you about an hour or so before dark. Now he's not the big bear, but he's a 'keeper' nonetheless. You watch intently as this 'keeper' fidgets around the bait, eventually turning broadside and giving you a perfect shot at his vitals. Should you shoot?

"If you truly want a big bear, the answer is absolutely not! You see, a dominant bear is probably in the wings, as evidenced by previous sightings, the 'keeper' bear's early arrival at the site and his apparent nervousness around the bait. An informed hunter would pass up the 'keeper' knowing full well that a record-book animal may indeed show himself just before dark."

How do you learn more about black bear behavior? "Aside from first-hand experience and talking extensively with successful hunters," adds Smith, "I recommend my clients read everything they can get their hands on and study every bear-hunting video that comes across their path. Like deer and deer hunting, I don't think you can ever know too much about the sport of hunting black bears!"

Eric Grinnell of Silvertip Outfitters is another camp owner who routinely gets bears for his clients. My friends and I have bagged five trophy bruins over the years with this Alberta outfitter, including three that tipped the scales over 400 pounds (see Chapter 10). When Grinnell talks bears, hunters should listen.

"Bear hunters book hunts with us in part because of

our expertise," says Grinnell. "That is, we have plenty of field experience and we know bears. Nonetheless, every so often, a hunter will pay for our services and then for one reason or another, not follow our advice.

"This happens on occasion when we think a bait should be left alone for a few days to allow a bear to become better acclimated to the site. Or when we put a hunter on a bait that is only being hit sporadically, but knowing that a real jumbo is working the area. If the hunter hunts the first stand anyways, he is not likely going to see that bear, only wise him up a bit. And if he refuses to hunt that 'dead' bait, he could miss out on an opportunity of a lifetime.

"We also caution our clients to be as quiet as possible approaching the stand in the evening and exiting the stand at dark. Take your time and tiptoe in and out with the utmost of caution. It is common enough to spook a bear off a bait when you are running a bait line, but usually the bear will return in a day or two if you give him half a chance. However, you want to avoid spooking a bear when you are actually hunting him.

"Bears learn quickly, especially big bears, and one mistake is all you get. In fact, if the bear knows he is being hunted and learns you are poking around 'his' area at prime time, he may very well go nocturnal or even avoid the bait site all together."

Mel Johnson, head guide for Zane Picowicz's Pierceland Outfitters in Pierceland, Saskatchewan, has been hunting and trapping black bears for almost 60 years. And during this time he has tagged over 600 bruins, more than anyone else in the province! What does he consider to be THE cardinal error in bear hunting?

"A bear has an excellent sense of smell," says Johnson, "but unlike a whitetail, a black bear often associates the smell of man with food. Thus human odor alone does not always spook a bear away from a bait station.

"A bruin's sense of hearing is also very good. In fact, it is much better than most hunters think, and a bear will be extremely cautious if he hears any unusual sounds around the bait. Thus you should certainly be quiet whenever you're in or near your treestand. However, like his sense of smell, a bear can come to associate certain sounds with food, too. Indeed, on some occasions just banging the bait barrel can bring a bear into rifle range."

What should hunters be most careful of then, human odors or man-made sounds? "You must play the wind and you must settle down once you climb into your treestand," says Johnson, "but the biggest mistake you can make is moving around. Bears have been known to return to the same bait a week or 10 days after being nicked with a bullet or arrow, but will rarely return once they've caught a glimpse of a restless man. Unlike human scent and man-made sounds, quick and

Narrowly gapped tooth impressions indicate a cub or yearling on the bait.

irregular movements spell d-a-n-g-e-r to a black bear."

That's why full camouflage is so important, including face and hands, no matter what weapon you choose to take afield. I know it is difficult to sit still for 4 or 5 hours at a time, especially when mosquitoes and black flies are buzzing about, but a good camouflage pattern will block your silhouette and minimize the effect of those involuntary movements we all seem to make.

"The act of shooting a gun or bow is very critical when it comes to bear hunting," adds Johnson, "because of the many gestures involved. As I said, a black bear's eyes are quick to pinpoint motion, and the movement it takes to raise a rifle or a bow can be a dead give-away to an alert bruin. Wait for the bear's attention to be riveted on food before attempting a shot."

Larry Buchberger and Bob Johnson of River Rat Outfitters specialize in gargantuan bruins along a lonely stretch of the Saskatchewan River in northern Manitoba. "The number one reason hunters don't see bears is that they don't sit still. They fidget with their bow, they crack the bolt on their rifles, they crane their necks to look behind them, they open and close their fanny packs—in short they move around as if they are watching television in their living room! A trophy boar will often camp out 100 yards or so from a bait site so he can keep tabs on 'his' food supply. Unusual sounds can force a big bear to go nocturnal.

"Another mistake hunters make is moving when they see a bear circling the bait site. A big bear often approaches very carefully and surveys the situation for some time before committing himself to the set-up. If he catches you moving your head for a better look-see, or repositioning your weapon, he'll be gone in a flash. You must sit still and be ready to shoot the moment you settle into the stand!"

Ray Broughton and his sons Peter and Perry from Newfoundland agree with Larry and Bob. "Each season we get a few bowhunters in camp who want to video tape their kill," say the Broughtons. "It's a great idea, but it so often ends in failure. Unless the bowhunter is an experienced cameraman and is willing to trade an actual kill for raw footage, we try to discourage it. Two people on a bait mean twice as much scent and twice as much movement. And that means twice the chance of being detected. More than one 'film maker' has gone home empty-handed because he moved to get a better 'shot' at a big bear."

Another problem bear hunters must learn to avoid is misjudging the size of the bear. It makes little difference if you are hunting over bait, spot-and-stalking open hillsides, still-hunting beech ridges, tracking them in the snow or running them with dogs, estimating the live weight of a black bear is a difficult endeavor. Mel Johnson once told me if he could slide the bear into a wheelbarrow, he was confident he could guess the weight of the bear within a few pounds. But if he could not get the bear in the wheelbarrow, all bets were off! "There is just too much fat and fur on a big bear," he told me!

So how do you know if the bear in front of you is a trophy bruin, a potential record-book "keeper?" Bob Heyde and Eric Grinnell both tell their clients to look for a boar, as most "book" bears are males. "Boars are well-muscled with large necks and powerful-looking shoulders, much like big-league football players," they argue. "If you have the time to look closely, you will also see a penile sheath, like that of a dog, a scarred face, from all the fighting they do, and legs that appear short and stocky. A big bear also has a wide butt and a belly that seems to drag on the ground and will approach a bait site very carefully, moving one foot at a time in a precise fashion. Put that all together and stir in a belligerent attitude, and you have a big male black bear in your sights!

"On the other hand, a sow will not be as careful with each step as she approaches any baited area, and her muscles are not as well defined. She will also have a wet spot under her tail whenever she urinates."

One mistake all the outfitters, guides and booking agents caution their hunters against is taking a shot from any angle that does not fully expose the vitals, be it with bow, rifle or muzzleloader. And that means waiting for the perfect broadside or quartering-away angle. A well-placed projectile in the vitals will result in a quick and humane kill. Any other angle is risky at best and almost always results in a lost bear.

Unless you are a professional photographer, avoid the impulse to video your own hunt. Your chances of success plummet dramatically whenever you bring a friend along to record the events.

Blood-Trailing Nasty Bruins

Looking for a wounded bear is not for the faint of heart!

Over the years, my friends and I have blood-trailed several wounded bears, mostly at night, always through the thickest tangles and only after first securing permission from the local game warden. We often surprised ourselves at just how close we would get to a downed bruin before we saw him piled up—even with the aid of several gas lanterns. Fortunately, all but one of the bears we tracked were dead on arrival. The one that wasn't scared the hell out of all of us.

It all started on the last day of the hunt. One of the gang had nailed a bear early in the evening, and although there was a good blood trail complete with scuffed-up leaves and broken branches, he was unable to locate the bruin. After we heard all the details (the angle of the shot, what the bear did when shot, the direction the bruin headed after the shot and so forth), we decided to grab one 12-gauge shotgun between us and pick up the trail. We were sure we would find the bear stone dead, but it looked like rain and we wanted to locate the bear before the downpour washed away the blood trail. Besides, we wanted to get back to camp before dark. It's no fun sharing the thick bush with hordes of biting insects after the sun goes down.

The blood trail was easy to follow, and we were almost tripping over each other in our excitement to be the first to spot the dead bear. Suddenly, the mortally wounded bruin stood up 10 yards in front of us and snarled. We all quickly jumped behind the man with the 12-gauge for protection. Charley wanted to pass the shotgun over to the young hunter, since it was his first bear, but he was standing too far back to do any good. So with our encouragement, Charley knocked the bruin down with one blast.

"I think he's about dead," someone said after a few moments of heavy breathing, but no one was ready to start skinning the big bear quite yet. The five of us, all standing behind the man with the gun, thought it wise to wait at least a few more minutes before anyone got too close. Finally, Charley went over and poked the bear, and sure enough, it had expired. That's when we found out the shotgun had jammed after that first shot! Talk about a false sense of security.

We later found that the bear had been shot through the liver. Even if it had rained, a body search at first light would have easily located the dead bear. It is incidents like these that have taught us to wait until morning to track a wounded bear whenever possible.

THE FIRST STEP

The easiest bears to track down are those that have been shot through both lungs. It makes little difference if you use a bow, muzzleloader or a modern firearm; a bear hit in the boiler room generally leaves a good blood trail and doesn't go far.

The first bear I ever tagged with archery tackle is a case in point. I watched the bear hit the bait two nights in a row. On his second visit to the pile of meat scraps in as many nights, I waited for the classic broadside angle before drilling him at less than 20 yards. The bear bellowed when the arrow struck and bolted for the brush with all four legs clawing at the ground like he was in four-wheel drive.

The bruin passed in front of me before suddenly turning and running uphill about 40 yards. There it collapsed behind the bait pile only a few yards from where I later found my arrow. A death moan soon reverberated through the bush and then all was quiet.

Discretion being the better part of valor, I grabbed my 12-gauge pump from behind the seat of the 4x4, loaded it and walked up on the bear. It was dead all right, but when I turned it over to see exactly where my arrow had struck, a bit of trapped air escaped from its lungs causing a loud hissing sound. I must have jumped 6 feet in the air!

The point is the bear was dead the moment the arrow

Watch out, he's still alive!

Examine arrow shafts and fletching carefully for evidence of hair and blood. The sign on this arrow indicates a solid hit.

passed through both lungs, and in its mad dash to escape, went nowhere and died within sight of me. I checked later, and that double-lung shot left an easy-to-read blood trail.

MARGINALLY HIT BRUINS

But what happens when the hit is not so solid? What should you do then? As with any big-game animal, you should keep all your senses riveted on the escaping bear, paying close attention to where the animal was hit and his direction of travel. Mark the spots where you last saw the bear and heard any sounds it may have made along his death route, such as crashing timber or splashing water, that might you help locate the dead bear later on. Then keep your ears open for additional sounds such as more breaking brush and, of course, the death rattle.

All this is important because a poorly hit bear, one that travels more than 150 to 200 yards after being shot, can be very difficult to recover. The blood trail is almost always sparse, partly because the fat on the bear tends to plug the entry and exit holes and partly because the thick hair tends to soak up any blood that does trickle out.

Now comes the tough part. You generally have to get on your hands and knees to look for specks of blood, scuffed-up leaves, bent or broken plants and soft impressions in the earth to help decipher the escape route. And if you shot

your bear just before dark, the task becomes even more difficult. Your job, however, is to put all the pieces of the puzzle together quickly and make a decision.

If the bear is already dead, you should have no problem finding him a short distance from your stand. If he is mortally wounded but still very much alive, you should back off and pick up the trail in the morning. If you jump him after the shot, he could disappear forever in the wilds, or he could turn and charge you.

Most experienced bear hunters will back away if they have any doubts about the hit. One year, a member of our hunting party arrowed a huge Pope and Young boar just before dark. He admittedly took a low percentage shot, electing to put an arrow between the bear's neck and front shoulder as the boar walked towards his treestand. He'll never do that again.

The bruin bolted for the bush as soon as the arrow struck and then circled through a clear-cut before stepping back into the thick bush. The blood trail was fairly good, indicating the arrow took out at least one lung, but the bear had gone almost 300 yards and was yet to be found.

At one point, Bob saw where the bear turned and

Bear blood trails are notoriously sparse.

Self-doubt can creep in when confronted with a bent arrow shaft and little blood.

Be careful!

entered a blowdown thick with alders and dead branches. He heard a low hissing sound followed by a few snapping twigs, and as he later told us back at camp, "I about passed out." Armed only with a dim flashlight and a stout bow, Bob quietly backed away and returned to camp.

He was still white as a ghost when he told us the story a few hours later. I had also arrowed a bear that evening, and we were all late getting back to the cabin. After discussing Bob's bear at length, we decided to pick up the blood trail right then and there rather than wait until first light. The air was thick with moisture, and we feared a heavy downpour would wash out the trail. After all, there is safety in numbers, isn't there?

When Bob showed us the blowdown, we all shivered a bit. It definitely was a scary hole and a perfect spot for an ambush. I slowly circled the tangle of logs and brush looking for an exit trail, but none was to be found. Not a single speck of blood! Surmising the bear was still in there, possibly still alive, we left and returned at first light.

And am I glad we did! We found the bear dead, but he was lying on his belly facing his back trail like grizzlies are known to do. The sounds Bob heard the evening before were probably the bear adjusting himself in his death bead, and if he had entered the blowdown,

the bear probably would have nailed him.

To add to the potential horror, Bob was alone and his exact whereabouts were unknown to us. If Bob had been attacked, we probably would not have been able to find him until first light. And by then it could have been too late.

Are there any lessons here? You bet! For starters, never take low-percentage shots. Two, never follow a blood trail more than 200 yards alone. And three, never follow a blood trail from a marginally hit bruin without adequate backup.

COMPLICATING ISSUES

The first problem you will encounter blood-trailing bruins, especially in poor light, is messing up the sign. Sometimes in our haste to recover the bruin, we simply get ahead of ourselves and in so doing step on crucial evidence. Blood specks can be obliterated by the soles of your boots, for example, and the vegetation you beat down can be indistinguishable from the plant stems the bear crushed. It is always best to take your time, pay attention to detail and mark the trail as you go.

The next problem is having too many helpers. Two or three is ideal, but four or more can be a real chore unless you are doing a body search the next day. All participants should be quiet and talk in low tones and even then only if absolutely necessary. Sound travels far on a quiet night, and a human voice will easily spook a nearby bruin further into the forest.

One spring we were blood-trailing a bruin that was thought to have expired close to the stand. As darkness settled in, however, we could not find hide or hair of the dead bruin, and as we continued our search, we drifted several hundred yards away from our parked 4x4s. Under these circumstances, it is easy to get turned around in the darkness. Fortunately, I had taken a compass bear-

You need all the help you can get when the trail runs cold.

ing before picking up the trail and found my way back to the truck and signaled the rest of the crew with the horn. Today, besides a compass and plenty of mosquito repellent, I carry an extra flashlight (trying to install a new bulb in the darkness is often an exercise in futility), flagging tape and either a whistle or a boat horn. And if we do have a fifth wheel, we position him at the bait site or the truck in case somebody needs help getting out of the bush.

What happened to that bear? Well, he doubled back just like my first archery kill and expired within sight of the stand. We found him the next morning.

ALLERGIC TO LEAD

Your number one concern while on the trail of a wounded bear, especially after dark, is having a loaded firearm in your midst. One of the first blood trails we ever followed was a bear skinned by an arrow just before sundown. The blood was sparse, so we decided to give the bear time to bleed out before we resumed tracking. We returned to camp, made a quick call to the warden and then each of us grabbed either a shotgun or a lever-action 30-30.

That night was a nightmare for all of us, for not only were we looking for a wounded bear—a bear, by the way, we never recovered—but each of us was also concerned for everyone else's safety. We didn't want to have a run in with a wounded bear nor did we want to accidentally shoot each other if the bear suddenly became aggressive. It was almost

a no-win situation.

The potential for a disaster was emotionally draining. However, the experience taught us to cut down on the number of guns when trailing wounded bears. Now only one man totes a firearm, and everyone else stays out

Wounded bears have been known to make a wallow. Conventional wisdom tells us the bears pack the wound with mud in an effort to stop the bleeding. The cool mud also seems to soothe their temperament. Are black bears really that smart?

of his way. He must have a cool head and only shoot if necessary. Through the years, there have only been two occasions when we actually had to use firepower, and both times we were glad we had it. However, there have been several other episodes where we wished we had adequate backup and didn't.

Be extra careful approaching any wounded animal, especially a large fur ball with teeth and claws.

Take compass bearings before you pick up the blood trail.

Two expert bear hunters helped me find this Pope and Young bruin, Bob Heyde and his uncle, Jake Newfeld, of Homestead outfitters.

Black Bear Backup

Only one out of a hundred bears will give you cause for concern. The problem is you don't know if it is the first bear you run across, the 52nd bear you meet or number 90. Darth Vader gave me the creeps. It was situated on high ground at the end of an esker, several miles from the nearest unimproved dirt road. The esker, shaped like a hog's back, was thick with spruce trees, some as big as my thigh, that seemed to grow at grotesque angles to the game trail that ran its entire length, ending abruptly along the shores of an impenetrable mosquito-infested swamp deep in the Canadian bush. Even at noon on a cloudless day, the trail was full of dark shadows, requiring at times the yellow beam of a flashlight to help illuminate the path.

I never went down that trail without some sort of personal protection. At first I shouldered a full-size axe, but later, once the bait started disappearing, I began toting a lever-action 45/70, and I never found it to be too much gun for the circumstances. The swamp was, after all, an ideal location for a mature black bear, the kind of bear that will hold its ground despite your intrusion. And the kind of bear that goes "woof" in the dark.

For a week, the honey and assorted foodstuffs I left at the end of the esker went untouched. Then one afternoon I discovered the barrel of goodies had been disturbed. At first I thought it might have been ravens or wolves, but upon closer inspection I discovered several curly black strands of hair caught on the bait barrel, which indicated a bear was working the area.

I tossed some more food onto the bait pile and left to check the rest of my baits. I then waited for a couple of days before sneaking back in for a quick look-see. This time the bait was gone—all of it. I knew that unless spooked, the bear would eventually return again and again, so I quickly erected a portable stand downwind of the bait barrel and carefully exited the site.

My goal was to make sure there was always plenty of food in and around the barrel and to let the bruin feed relatively undisturbed until I could learn more about him. I have shot several good bears over the years, including a half dozen that tipped the scales between 300 and almost 500 pounds on the pad. I wanted my next bruin to be of that caliber.

A week later, after carefully examining the bear sign around the rest of the bait line, I sat over the Darth Vader for the first time. As if on cue, a huge Pope and Young bruin appeared just before darkness set in and approached the set-up with little hesitation. I confidently sent an arrow at that book blackie a few moments later when he stuck his head inside the bait barrel. The big bruin growled and banged his head on the barrel before he exited the scene like a scalded dog. His quick escape was to no avail, however, as he was already dead on his feet. I found him piled up less than 50 yards distant.

WHY PACK A GUN?

There was a time I toted a loaded pump shotgun each time I replenished a bait site, but it soon became cumbersome to load and unload it at every station. Then I started carrying a single-bit axe with me, thinking I could swing it if need be in self-defense. Well, those days are over, too. The axe is worthless against an enraged black bear, but a firearm is always handy should you encounter a black bear with an attitude—if you take the time to carry it every time you expect an encounter.

But let's face the facts. Any big-game animal that you choose to pursue today in North American can kill you. A bugling bull elk, for instance, will go after just about anybody that gets too close to one of his cows, and rutting bull moose have been known to charge locomotives. Indeed, we have all heard stories of how a "dead" whitetail buck suddenly stood up and raced blindly towards his attacker, and we all know what a grizzly sow will do if she feels her cubs are in danger. Even the lowly wild boar will give you a run for your money if he senses you getting a little too close for comfort.

It is the black bear, however, that probably accounts

A wounded bear is a very dangerous animal. Pack a gun!

for more bites and clawings today, if for no other reason than it is our number two big-game animal. There are lots of hunters in the bush chasing black bears these days, not to mention campers, tourists and fishermen, making bear-human contacts nearly unavoidable in some areas. Indeed, black bears make great bow targets, and the fact that they can kill a full-grown moose with one swipe of a forepaw simply adds to the adventure.

Over the years, I have had plenty of bears stop me in my tracks. A young boar for example kept me pinned in my treestand one evening until the outfitter came along and shooed him away. That bear was quite aggressive, however, and for the next several evenings, he followed me out of the woods by staying in the brush 10 or 12 yards behind me. I thought we were going to have to pop him with a gun before someone got hurt, but he finally left the scene.

I have also had several bears stand on their hind legs next to my stand for a better look-see, and two have actually climbed up the tree sniffing and woofing all the way. A harsh word was all it took to send them packing though.

It is the wounded bears, however, that can really make you question your sanity. One year, a pal and I were blood-trailing a big boar when the outfitter handed me his 30-30. He had to get on his hands and knees to look for blood, and he told me to shoot the bear if it charged. I looked down the barrel and saw that the front blade sight was bent horribly to the left. I asked him where the rifle shot. His answer gave me goose bumps. "I don't know," he told me, "I never shot it before!"

Other outfitters that offered firepower for backup have also given me cause for concern. One had his 12

Ask your outfitter if he has adequate backup in camp. If not, bring your own.

gauge loaded with No. 4 bird shot while another had to use a hammer to open the action on his rusted British 303. Yet another was such a poor shot, he couldn't hit a 4'x8' sheet of plywood at 50 yards!

I have had enough bad experiences that today, after bowhunting bears for 30 years or so, I now supply my own backup. In fact, I often tote it right to the treestand "just in case" I run into an aggressive bruin at the bait pile or have to track down a poorly hit bear by myself in the near darkness, as I had to do several years ago. Fortunately, that bear was DOA, but horror stories abound of hunters who pursued arrow-hit bruins only to find an angry ball of teeth and fur waiting in ambush.

A high-powered rifle is a measure of safety when bowhunting western bruins.

FIVE GOOD CHOICES

What makes a good backup weapon for black bears? The most common choice is a 12-gauge pump fitted with open fiber optic sights. My Ithaca Deerslayer II loaded with Winchester slugs, for example, will make quick work of any angry bruin. It is quick and easy to shoot, and if need be, just about anybody can squeeze off a shot on your behalf.

A large caliber high-powered rifle is also a good choice, especially if you are on a two-species hunt such as moose/bear or elk/bear. In these cases, I carry one of four lightweight lever-actions with me. Not only will any one of them body-slam a big bear if need be, each is also capable of downing a moose or elk in a pinch. Like the Ithaca Deerslayer II, they are quick to point and nearly foolproof in times of need.

Winchester's big-bore Model 94 chambered in the 356 Winchester pushes a 200-grain flat-nosed pill from the muzzle at 2460 fps, delivering 2688 foot-pounds of energy at point-blank range. I installed a large Lyman peep sight on mine for better aiming at close range.

Marlin's "Guide Gun," the 1895G chambered for the venerable 45/70 Government, is a good second choice. It weighs only 7 pounds and features an 18 1/2-inch ported barrel. Factory ammo in a standard 22-inch barrel with a 405-grain bullet generates 1330 fps and 1590 foot-pounds of energy at the muzzle. The shorter barrel is 75-100 fps less.

My third choice is the Marlin 1895M in the new 450 Marlin caliber. Like the Guide Gun, it too sports an 18-1/2 inch ported barrel and is easy to swing in tight situations. This gun is a real banger. It generates a 2100 fps muzzle velocity with a 350-grain bullet and over 3400 foot-pounds of energy—which is more than enough firepower for a black bear.

The ultimate black bear backup, however, is undoubtedly a Winchester 1886 converted to the 50 Alaskan by the well-known gunsmith Doug Turnbull. This is a gun that pushes a 500-grain bullet around 2000 fps, creating about 4000 foot-pounds of energy!

After converting a newly manufactured Winchester, Turnbull spruces up the lever action by offering several options that include new wood, fancy checkering, pistol grip, take-down or solid frame and shorter or longer barrels. The gun also comes with complete metal work to duplicate the turn-of-the-century metal finish, including rust bluing and, of course, his famous color case hardening. Conversions start at around $1200. For more information, contact Doug Turnbull Restorations, 6680 Routes 5-20, Bloomfield, NY 14469; (585)-657-6338; www.turnbullrestoration.com.

So if you are in need of a backup for black bear, and every bear camp should have at least one, any of these guns should do the trick.

Just don't be afraid to use it!

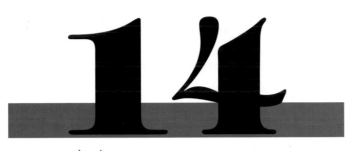

Taxidermy

What you do in the field can make all the difference in the world!

On my last night in Newfoundland, I chose to hunt Kitty's Brook, a bait site that was being hit on an intermittent basis. Both Ray and I believed there was a good bear in the vicinity, although there were no tracks or scat to bolster that opinion.

Ten minutes before dark, a sow, accompanied by a 425-pound boar, circled the bait and stepped into the opening. I pulled back my High Country Extreme, but "Romeo" suddenly lay down next to a huge log, protecting his vitals from all but the very best aimed arrow. I eased back on the string and waited.

A few minutes later, the boar stood up to lick some honey off that log. I came to full draw again, but this time the sow walked in next to the boar. If I had shot then, my compound would have undoubtedly sent a shaft through both bears, and even though there was a two-bear limit in Newfoundland, I elected not to take the sow. I eased up on the string again and waited.

Suddenly, Romeo walked off the bait and into the shadows. I was flabbergasted. After all that time, after passing up multiple bruins during the previous two weeks, including five that would have probably made the book, I was going home skunked. I couldn't help but snicker at myself for being so choosy. Nonetheless, I settled down and waited. There was still a minute or so of legal shooting light left.

Without warning, the boar suddenly came back into view and stood behind the bait with his near fore leg fully extended. I quickly picked a spot, brought my bow to full draw and released an Easton Aluminum XX75 2514 tipped with a 100-grain Thunderhead at his vitals. The bear lurched and scampered off 30 yards or so and then walked slowly into the underbrush.

I immediately got down and looked for blood. It was everywhere! After a sleepless night, Ray Broughton and his two sons Peter and Perry followed me back to the bait site where we found the Pope and Young bruin

piled up less than 75 yards away. It was the perfect end to a perfect hunt.

MISTAKES TO AVOID

There are few mounts more impressive than a life-size black bear. Standing tall or walking on all fours, a "stuffed" black bear dresses up any trophy room with grace and awe. Indeed, my living room and den are loaded with a half-dozen fully mounted bears plus a half bear and several bear rugs and tanned skins. There are also several bleached and "de-bugged" bear skulls scattered about the place. They certainly grab your attention when you enter the room.

Unfortunately, some taxidermists cut corners when they attempt to bring a mature bruin back to life. One Saskatchewan outfitter/taxidermist, for example, hacked nearly 9 inches of hide off a chocolate Pope & Young bear I arrowed in his camp. Why? "Mike" simply did not want to spend the extra time creating a form big enough to fit my bear, and unbeknownst to me, shortened the hide with an old knife. He was too busy, after all, doing hunting videos and entertaining celebrities in his camp to make good on his word. It's too bad I paid him in advance. His truck had broken down while I was in camp, and he begged me for the money upfront.

When I saw the finished product, my blood pressure went through the ceiling, and I felt betrayed. My 79-inch nose-to-tail boar was now 70 inches in length. The damage was so severe even another taxidermist could not make any corrections. Once the sewing is complete and the hide glued to the form, you are stuck with the finished product, like it or not.

Another life-size bear from a different taxidermist came back to me with several claws damaged or missing. Apparently, the hide was put in a commercial dryer to remove excess moisture, and the claws were slammed against the metal drum as the hide was rolled over and over and over again. Aside from legal action, which will

The pelt of a mature boar is so luxurious, it begs for you to do something special to preserve it.

Take as many measurements as you can before you start skinning.

cost you plenty and not bring the hide back to its natural state, you are stuck. Paint and putty camouflaged most of the damage, but anybody who looks at the claws knows there is something wrong with them.

Yet another bear mount, this one a half-bear, also left me with a bad taste in my mouth. The hide cracked and split on the form after only a couple of years of hanging in my den. Fortunately, the damage is not readily visible, except to me. It could have been worse, however. A friend of mine had a half-bear's hide come alive with insects a few months after he got it home. He noticed an unusual smell, but the taxidermist assured him the mount was in good shape and that the odor would soon disappear. Well, it didn't; the hide was never properly tanned, and the bad odor was the hide rotting on the form. The half-bear ended up in the dump.

So what can you do to avoid being ripped off? How can you avoid the problems I have experienced? The first step is to never, ever, ever leave your bear hide with a taxidermist whose workmanship and reputation is unknown to you. This includes buddies of the outfitter and out-of-state taxidermists who are willing to give you a cut-rate deal because they "know what a bear from these parts is supposed to look like." If you cave in, as I have, you are just asking for trouble.

Never leave your hide in a foreign country, either. It took me 3 years to get a salted hide out of Canada and home. Twice the bear was in the US, but red tape kept it from being flown to my hometown. I could not drive 200 miles to pick it up, either, because a Fish and Wildlife Officer had to inspect the hide, and there was no officer in the city where the hide was being stored. And no, I could not have the hide commercially transported by rail or truck to the officer because, you guessed it, the hide had not been inspected. Lost paper work, airline snafus and more red tape kept that hide in limbo for years. If not for the help of the local U.S. Fish and Wildlife Officer, that hide would still be in an airline container somewhere between Canada and the United States.

THINK AHEAD

There is, of course, no guarantee you will score on a fair-chase black bear hunt. But you should be optimistic and think about how you would like to have your trophy mounted just in case. "You shouldn't just start skinning your bear," says Tracy Hodge, a noted taxidermist from Batavia, New York, "without first making some hard decisions. Do you want a life-size bear or a bear rug in your living room? What about a half-mount, which is a good choice if the hindquarters of your bear's hide have been 'rubbed?'"

Black bear hides require special handling in the field, not the least of which are skinning the animal properly and taking the necessary steps to temporarily preserve the hide until you can get it to your taxidermist. If you are not sure how to do this, take the time to visit a couple of local taxidermists who are knowledgeable about black bear hides before you embark on your hunt. Unlike a poorly worked deer head, where another hide can be purchased to show off the antlers, your bear hide is one-of-a kind; you can't get another. If the ears look funny, or the nose is out of joint, or the mouth is crooked, all you can do is grit your teeth and learn to live with it.

Should you take any measurements before you start skinning your bear? Taxidermists differ in opinion on this. Tracy Hodge prefers to take the measurements himself off the green hide whereas two other taxidermists, Rick Streeter from Ontario, New York, and Rick Plant

Decide how you want your bear hide to be mounted—full, half or on a rug—before you start skinning.

On a hot day, photograph your bear as soon as possible and then skin it out. The clock of decomposition begins the very second the bear expires.

from Fairport, New York, want the hunter to take his own measurements before any skinning takes place. They recommend you measure from the nose to base of tail and the circumference of his chest just behind the front legs. "I like to take my own measurements," says Hodge, "because some guys get excited and 'stretch' the hide a bit in an effort to make their bear look bigger. In other words, they want me to make their 150-pound sow look like a 250-pound boar, and frankly, that's impossible."

LIFE-SIZE MOUNT

"If you decide to have your bear mounted life-size," advises Hodge, "then you must skin the bear out properly. First slit the bear up the belly from rectum to sternum, leaving his sex organs intact. Run your knife just under the skin, using your fingers as a guide, and try not to puncture the stomach. Then start peeling the hide back leaving as much fat, meat and tissue on the body of the bear as possible.

"Next, beginning at that initial incision, split each leg all the way down the inside. When you get to the feet, split the hide from the middle of the heel to the middle of the main pad, stopping at the toes. This gives me plenty of opportunity to hide the incisions when it comes time for me to sew the hide onto the bear form. I will have to split them anyways when it comes time to work the hide around the threaded rod molded into the poly form. The

rods are used to fasten the finished mount to the base with bolts, nuts and washers. Finally, cut the foot off at the 'ankle,' and let your taxidermist remove the hide from the rest of the foot and toes in his studio.

"Unless you are experienced, do not cape out the head of your bear," cautions Hodge. "The hair is short on the nose and face, and any mistake(s) you make in the skinning process are difficult to repair. Just pull the hide forward to the base of the bear's skull, and cut off the head with a knife by inserting the blade between two vertebrae."

BLACK BEAR RUG

"If you have your heart set on a black bear rug, they you follow the same general skinning pattern," says Hodge, "except you must be very careful to preserve uniformity. When you are splitting the hide up the belly and down each leg for example, you must be mindful and make both sides even and proportional to each other. A taxidermist can only do his best job with a properly prepared skin. If you want the left side of the finished rug to look just like the right side, then wield the knife attentively or the taxidermist may have to cut away some fur from the side with 'too much hide.'

"You now have the choice of bringing the hide to your taxidermist as soon as possible or freezing the hide unsalted. When I get the hide, I prefer to measure the green hide myself, after fleshing, and then send the hide

You'll cut fewer holes in the hide with a sharp knife.

Black bear hides are very greasy and must be fleshed as soon as possible and definitely before salting.

to a commercial tannery for processing. There will be some shrinkage after the tanning is complete, but when the hide comes back to my shop, it is still pliable enough for me to stretch it back to the original measurements. When I am done, the mount should be the same size as the bear you shot."

DO-IT-YOURSELF HUNT

If you prefer to hunt on your own, then you must be prepared to handle all the taxidermy chores in camp. That means you cannot lollygag about camp. Get your photographs of the bear as soon as possible and then skin the animal quickly. The clock of decomposition starts the very second the bear expires, and on a warm sunny day—75 degrees and above—time is of the essence.

Rick Streeter is an award-winning taxidermist with a penchant for detail who, like Hodge and Plant, believes you must be prepared to take care of your trophy before it hits the ground. "On any do-it-yourself hunt," advises Streeter, "check ahead to see if there will be a generator in camp for cooling the hide and meat. Is there a freezer available in a nearby town? What about a walk-in cooler? A taxidermist? A meat cutter? If the answer to any of these questions is 'no,' then you must be prepared to make other arrangements before you step into the field.

"Even if you book a fully guided trip, you can't expect the outfitter or guide to double as an expert taxidermist, too. I just had a new client come into my studio requesting a full body mount on a beautiful black bear. Unfortunately, his guide cut the bear's rear legs off, and there is nothing I can do to repair the damage."

If you are back in the boonies and do not have access to a freezer or cooler, then you are going to have to remove the skull yourself, but be careful. As Hodge said, the hairs are quite short in this area, making it difficult for a taxidermist to repair the damage if you cut a hole or lop off an ear by mistake. Use a scalpel, available through your taxidermist, or a small folding knife, the smaller and sharper the better. Use a larger knife only for scraping excess meat off the hide.

Take your time and do a good job. What you do in the field before it reaches a taxidermist can mean the difference between a life-like mount for your living room wall or a bad mount destined for the back of the garage.

"The first mistake hunters make when caping a black bear," says Streeter, "is cutting into the membrane located right above each eyeball. What we get here at the studio is a cape with four eyeholes. To make sure this doesn't happen to you, stick your finger into the animal's eye socket and feel for the knife's blade. The presence of your finger

Skin the bear fully and then salt the entire hide. Do not freeze a salted hide.

against the blade will hopefully guide you around the socket and stop you from cutting through the upper eyelid.

"The second most common error occurs when you slice the lip, leaving most of it attached to the skull and not the hide. The trick here is to insert your finger inside the animal's mouth and find the knife's blade. Then cut inward and back towards the base of the jaw so that you do not cut across the lips. Your taxidermist will need at least a half-inch of lip all the way around in order to give you a quality, realistic-looking mount.

"Finally, when you get to the nose, stick your finger inside one nostril at a time (you can use a pair of rubber gloves here if you are a bit squeamish) and feel for the blade. You want to leave the animal's nose on the hide, not the skull.

"If you are going to be in the field for an extended period of time, and there is no freezer available, you must also turn the ears and split the lips. The lips are easy, but the ears are a bit tricky. I recommend to my clients they practice on whitetail deer before planning a do-it-yourself black bear hunt."

How should you transport the cape? Whenever possible pack the cape in a burlap bag. This will allow air to circulate around the hide. Generally, however, airlines want the hide in a plastic bag so that it doesn't leak blood into the hold of the aircraft. The second you disembark get your hide out of that plastic bag and into a burlap bag.

"You can also elect to transport your cape in an ice chest," says Streeter. "Put the ice in a plastic bag, or keep a block of ice in the bottom of the chest with a piece of burlap used to separate the hide from the melting ice and the bacteria in it."

If you don't want to chance skinning out the head yourself, it is best to freeze the cape and head. The cold temperatures will slow down the growth of bacteria and the deeper the freeze, the slower the growth.

"Do not salt and then freeze the cape, however," warns Streeter. "It will actually rot in the freezer, although at a slow rate. Like ice on a winter road, the hide will remain damp even though the air temperature in the freezer is well below freezing. If you do elect to freeze the cape, put it in a plastic bag. This is the only time, other than travelling on a commercial airplane when it is mandatory, that I would recommend the use of a plastic bag. You don't want a warm hide to sit in a pool of water where bacteria are thriving.

"Finally, look at a strand of bear fur under a microscope and you will see roots growing around each strand of hair. The bacteria loosen the roots causing the hairs to fall out. When packing, storing or transporting hides, think dry and cold. Moisture and warmth are big no-nos."

SALTING HIDES

Black bear hides are very greasy and must be fleshed as soon as possible, and certainly before the hide is salted. "Flesh down to the blue line," advises Rick Plant, "without cutting through the skin. That's when you are at the base of the hair roots. The better you can prepare the hide in this manner, the less chance of any damage or slippage later on." Indeed, this is why you leave as much tissue on the bear's body as possible when skinning. Fleshing is hard work!

But why use salt to preserve the hide? "Salt is used to draw moisture out of the hide so that it dries; the theory being that bacteria needs moisture to survive," says Streeter. "Sometimes we see where a hunter salted the hide out to the head, but left the hide on the animal's skull. Invariably the mount is ruined because the unsalted portion of the hide spoiled.

"To salt a hide or cape properly, rub salt into the entire hide, paying close attention to the edges and the eyes, lips, ears and mouth on the head. Roll up the hide and store it in a cool area. Wait 24 hours, and shake out the wet salt. Then re-salt the hide and hang it out of the sunlight in a cool dark area. Your goal is to get all the wetness out of the hide."

I like to save some of that wet salt. It adds a spicy tang to my morning bear steak and eggs. (Just kidding!) Always use a fine-grained evaporated salt, which is available at most hardware or feed stores. Never use rock salt, and never try to freeze the hide after it has been salted.

"Once the hide is salted," adds Hodge, "do not transport it in a plastic bag or an air-tight container, as the hide will sweat, promoting bacterial growth and then slippage. Use a cardboard box, burlap bag, nylon sand bag or any other container that promotes air flow."

BEAR ESSENTIALS

You must be ready to handle the expected as well as the unexpected on any bear hunt. For skinning and caping, pack a scalpel knife or a small knife with a 4-inch blade, a fleshing knife with a 6-inch upsweeping blade, large snippers for cutting off feet and either a sharpening stone or a pair of sharpening sticks to keep all those blades sharp.

If the hide just needs to be kept cool, you will need a large airtight cooler with ice and a couple of burlap or other airflow-style bags. Do not put the hide in a plastic bag.

If your hide needs to be salted, one 80-pound bag of evaporated salt will be enough for two large bears. To transport the hide, use a burlap bag, canvas sea bag, wooden crate or other airflow-style container.

For meat storage, you will need a narrow-bladed boning knife, a medium to large meat knife with a straight to slightly curved blade, ice and a large airtight cooler.

If you think your bear might make one of the books, do not boil the skull; have it "bugged" instead.

OPTIONS, OPTIONS AND MORE OPTIONS— THE FINISHED MOUNT

A prime black bear hide is thick and luxurious, and common sense tells us to do something special with it. Indeed, black bears are probably the most unique animal in this regard because you can put them in all sorts of interesting, exotic poses.

"Unlike a deer mount where you are severely limited to a half-dozen or so standard poses," says Plant, "you can let your imagination run wild when you get ready to display a black bear hide.

"If money is an issue or you don't have a large room for a full mount, then a bear rug with a shell head and open mouth (we don't use the real skull or teeth) can be an impressive way to display your trophy. Another option is to do a half-bear mount with a snarling face, and display it as if it is coming through the wall. A few porcupine quills stuck in his snout will definitely add some meaning to the scene.

"Of course, nothing beats a full mount. You can do your bear standing with his mouth open, a popular pose, or you can add some action by having him swatting at a bee's nest. You can also have him standing over another animal mount, like a caribou head, as if he is protecting a recent kill.

"The sky is the limit when mounting a bear on all fours, too. Adding tree branches or logs to the base and then raising a paw off the ground can add action and a bit of realism to the pose. You can also have him scooping a brook trout out of a stream or fighting off a pair of coyotes! You can even do two bears locked in mortal combat, jaws agape!"

In my home, I have bears standing tall and on all fours. My favorites, however, include a cinnamon bear standing over a fly rod and basket full of mounted brook trout, as if he just ran the fisherman off, and a huge boar ripping apart a log full of honey, complete with dripping honey and freeze-dried honey bees. My next full-size mount now in the works will be a trophy boar about to step on the pan of a sharp-toothed bear trap!

"Finally, we can use everything but the growl when it comes to displaying a hard-earned trophy," adds Plant. "You can make a necklace from the claws or canine teeth and save patches of fur for your fly-tying buddies. You can even bleach the skull and have an Indian design painted on the brow."

Yes sir, when it comes time to add a black bear to your den, you are only limited by your imagination!

Streeter's Taxidermy
2287 Rt. 104
Ontario, NY 14519
315-524-0020

Rick's Taxidermy
15 Buckwheat Dr.
Fairport, NY 14450
585-377-5695

Triple "T" Taxidermy
20 Swan St.
Batavia, NY 14020
585-344-4928

RECORD-BOOK SKULLS

Nearly all book bears are boars, but not every boar makes the book. To learn if your big bear is big enough to qualify for any of the various record books, first clean the skull by careful boiling or by having it "bugged" by dermestid or carrion beetles at a commercial cleaner, which is the preferred method of museums and medical facilities.

I now favor the latter because it does not shrink the skull, soften the bone or otherwise damage the skull by over-boiling. Indeed, many big bears that would have otherwise made the book are disqualified because the front teeth are lost during the "cooking" process. This can cause a loss of about 3/16 of an inch from the total score. (If you can find the teeth, save them. They can be re-inserted back into the jaw later for scoring purposes.)

Those who boil their bear skulls also like to use a knife to cut away meat and gristle from the bone. Unfortunately, they often cut away the soft bone to get at the cartilage at the base of the skull. This loss can drop the total score below any of the club's minimum requirements.

After the skull has dried for 60 days at room temperature and room humidity, it is ready to be taken to an official measurer. He will use a set of calipers to gauge the length and the width of the skull. A minimum of 18 inches,

obtained by adding the length and the width of the skull together, is required for the Pope & Young Club whereas a minimum tally of 21 inches is needed for the coveted Boone & Crockett Club.

THE BONES BOUTIQUE
20 Swan
Batavia, New York 14020
585-344-4928

SKULLS UNLIMITED
10313 South Sunny Lane
Oklahoma City, OK 73160
1-800-659-7585

FINAL THOUGHTS ON PRESERVING YOUR TROPHY

- When skinning, try to leave as much muscle tissue on the carcass as possible. If you don't, your taxidermist will be spending extra hours later scraping the meat and fat off the hide. And those extra hours can cost you extra money.
- Some taxidermists are now using high-pressure water hoses to blow the fat off the hide.
- Many wildlife agencies demand you fork over a tooth for study. The information gathered will give them a better understanding of current population dynamics. It is usually a pre-molar, and its loss will in no way affect the final score of your bear's skull or the quality of your mount.
- Do not ever leave the entire skull with any individual or agency, however, as damage can occur. I left one skull in Newfoundland several years ago for "research," and when it was eventually returned to me, all the front teeth were missing! My letter of complaint to the biologist went unanswered, and I never got the teeth back. I will never loan them another skull.
- Your full body mount will not look bigger than the bear did in real life. In fact, due to hide shrinkage and the difficulty the taxidermist might have fitting the hide to a form, the bear may even look a tad smaller—but not much! That's because bear forms do not come in as many standard sizes as deer forms do, which means your taxidermist may have to add or delete certain sections of the form to help make the hide fit. Remember, it takes the eye of an artist and the heart of an outdoorsman to make the project come together in a pleasing form.

The Future of Bear Hunting:
Have We Lost It?

There is no doubt the anti-hunting movement feels bear hunting, both with dogs and over bait, is the soft underbelly of the American sportsman. To be sure, we are regularly attacked in the press as well as in the halls of our state and provincial governments for pursuing black bears in this manner. Even other hunters, who should know better, sometimes side with the anti-hunters on these issues. Why? Because so often they are not bear hunters!

I recently asked a wide array of experts their thoughts on bears and bear hunting and what the future holds for the sport. Is interest waning? What should we be doing to preserve our heritage? Their comments are worth reading twice.

"Bear numbers are on the rise, and success rates are going up. I think bear hunting, given the success of California's current management programs, will only get better." – Jon Kayser, outfitter.

"There will always be bears and bear hunting, but we must be vigilant. In the not too distant future, most prime hunting grounds will be leased to hunting clubs, leaving the average hunter scratching his head looking for a place to hunt." – Doug Turnbull, gunsmith and restorer of fine weapons.

"I fear California houndsmen will eventually lose the right to hunt black bears just as they have lost the right to hunt mountain lions. Today, we have government hunters trying to keep mountain lion populations in check. The sad part is that unbeknownst to the public, they are pursuing cats at the taxpayer's expense. Licensed dog owners should be playing a role here and putting money back into wildlife programs." – Brannon Byrne, independent houndsman.

"We have good bear populations in New York and good bear habitat, and we are always going to have good bear populations and good bear habitat. There will also always be a need to manage black bear populations, and the best way to control black bear populations is through regulated hunting." – Lou Berchielli, black bear biologist for the state of New York.

"We have lots of bears today, but too many tags in one area can hurt the resource. Nonetheless, given wise management, bear hunting in Manitoba should be good for decades to come." – Larry Buchberger and Bob Johnson, outfitters.

"The anti-hunters will never stop the hunt. There are simply too many powerful people who enjoy hunting, even though they do not acknowledge it in public. There will, however, always be an opposing opinion, as there is in everything." – Joe Quinn, former deputy sheriff, Westmoreland County, Pennsylvania.

"Most bear hunters are quiet souls. But if we get trampled on too much, the silent majority will no longer be silent." – Jim Utterback, former Constable for the state of Pennsylvania.

"There's no magic to tagging a bear, just hard work. Once a hunter gets one, he'll tell himself, 'Wow, I know how to do it!' Then he'll want a bigger bear, and with any luck, he'll be hooked for life." – Allen Miraglia, proprietor Scrubby Buck Archery Shop.

"Ontario's experiences were a godsend. We got organized, completed economic impact studies and identified the enemy. We are not fighting a losing battle here in Manitoba, we're winning the battle." – Jack Smith, outfitter.

"The closing of Ontario's spring bear season was a wake-up call. Today, Alberta black bear populations look good, and I'm optimistic about the future of bear hunting." – Eric Grinnell, outfitter.

"This government is very supportive of hunting, as evidenced by the recent passage of the Hunting and Fishing Heritage Act. Only time will tell if the (Ontario) spring bear season will ever be reinstated. There are many issues that need to be first examined, including tourism, economic impact, social issues and ethics." – Marie de Almeida, bear biologist for the Province of Ontario.

"There are not as many bear hunters as there are deer hunters. Now, if a state holds a public referendum on bear hunting, the outcome may be to outlaw baiting or the use of dogs. It is not that the anti-hunters won the ballot, just that many of those who voted were simply not bear hunters. In this scenario, success rates drop and hunter recruitment falls away. To manage increasing bear populations, states will then offer more bear tags valid during the regular big-game season. The end result of that referendum will be sportsmen will no longer be hunting bears specifically, but rather tagging bears as targets of opportunity." – Dave Garshelis, bear biologist for the state of Minnesota.

"There will always be people who like to hunt, but abhor bear hunting. They don't like the fact that you are killing bears just for the hide. Do you want to save bear hunting? Then eat bear meat!" – Steve Lamboy, former vice-president of Realtree.

"Experienced bear hunters here in Minnesota are after the meat, hides are secondary." – Dave Garshelis, bear biologist for the state of Minnesota.

"Interest in bears and bear hunting is on the rise. Many hunters, however, don't know where to go for a quality hunt." – Rick Plant, taxidermist.

"You really don't know anything about bears and bear hunting until you've sat quietly alone in bear country. The mere snapping of a twig is enough to unnerve anybody. Indeed, I have had hunters return to camp vowing never to hunt bears again because they just experienced the fright of their life. I have not, however, had a hunter return to camp after shooting a bear and tell me that hunting over bait is tame and unethical. Having a black bear within arm's reach, an animal that can so easily kill you, is a super rush for the real outdoorsman. Oh, I should say real outdoors person as more and more women are hunting bears these days. In fact, my wife loves it!" —Jeff Grab, booking agent.

"Most hunters only want to tag one bear in their lifetime, but there is a core group of bear hunters who look forward to hunting bears every year. They want to tag a bigger bear or one with an off-color hide." – Tracy Hodge, taxidermist.

"When we stop at a bear-check station, we very seldom see a teenager in the crowd. If we are going to beat the anti-hunters and save bear hunting, we have to get our youth involved in the sport." – Marvin and Karen Vought, officers, Physically Challenged Bowhunters of America, Inc.

"Bear hunters are a small group. Even if we don't agree on how our neighbor hunts, as long as it is a legal hunt, a traditional hunt, we should be supporting him." — Rick Streeter, taxidermist.

"The need to manage bear populations will always exist. The opportunities available to sportsmen will depend on their resolve to be an active participant in the management process." – Don Plant, author of Beyond the Woods and Water.

"Here in Wisconsin we have a constitutional right to hunt and fish. It just passed by an overwhelming majority of 84 percent of the vote. Hunters here are also making efforts to improve their public image. Wisconsin Houndsmen Association, for example, recently picked up 35 tons of garbage off federal lands. I think it is safe to say bear hunting will be around for a long time in Wisconsin." – Kyle LaFond, bear biologist for the state of Wisconsin.

"There will always be a bear season simply because bears are a nuisance animal, and as such, they are potentially dangerous. As bear populations increase, especially in areas where bear seasons have been shut down, there will be more conflicts and more problems. Eventually, there will be enough public pressure put on state and provincial governments to open a hunting season." – Judd Cooney, outdoor writer, outfitter.

"Sportsmen are interested in black bears because a big boar is at least as cagey if not more so than any whitetail buck. Black bear hunting will therefore remain strong as long as black-bear habitat is not threatened by man." – Jeffery W. Seitzinger, M.D., Plastic Surgeon, Montgomery, Alabama.

"It is amazing how little the general public knows about black bears and the big woods. Politics and the actions of the ignorant will cause bear seasons to close here in the Adirondacks in ten to fifteen years." – Mark Eddy, guide.

What should we be doing to protect our bear-hunting heritage?

"Do you want to save bear hunting? Then wear fur. The trappers took it on the chin with all those anti-fur ad campaigns while the American sportsmen and sportswomen stood silent. For shame! We should have been trapping's biggest supporters!" – Bill Vaznis, outdoor writer.

"For most hunters it starts out as one for the den. I see 25 to 50 percent of our clients, however, turn into 'bear lifers.' I do not know what they do with eight full mounts, but I know several hunters who have that many in their home and they still come back each spring to hunt big bears." – Bob Heyde, outfitter.

"Black bear populations are at an all-time high. The future of bear hunting, however, will not be decided on biology, but politics. There is no doubt in my mind we lose our right to bear hunt if we do not become politically active." – Bob Robb, outdoor writer and Alaskan bear guide.

BECOMING POLITICALLY ACTIVE . . .

Many people work behind the scenes in the political arena. One of their goals is to help get the word out on impending legislation that could have a negative impact on hunting, fishing or trapping. They also help organize meetings, write letters and work the phones for pro-hunting events. These guys and gals are the unsung heroes of the pro-hunting movement.

Unfortunately, there are also many high-profile people in the entertainment, corporate and sports arenas who could do much to promote the sport, but do not. They would rather duck the issue than have their public image "tainted" by any association with hunting, fishing, or trapping.

There is, however, one celebrity who spends enormous amounts of time and energy promoting hunting and icing the anti-hunters. Millionaire rock star Ted Nugent, with his quick wit and razor-tipped tongue, has been tireless in this regard.

Unlike most outdoor writers, magazine editors or the ubiquitous hunting video hot dogs who can only preach to the choir, Nugent gets a pro-hunting message across to millions of non-hunters. How? By using his music, an incredible sense of humor and his rapier wit to expose the anti-hunters for what they are—weenies.

Indeed, he regularly gives interviews extolling the virtues of hunting to non-hunting magazine writers, radio jocks and local television reporters. He also speaks the language to MTV viewers and adult talk show audiences like *The Late Show with David Letterman*. I've even seen him on the evening news discussing pirated music, and while doing so, he slyly mentions his hunting interests!

Here is an excerpt from his recent testimony before the New Jersey Fish and Game Council, given amidst a flurry of anti-hunting attacks by the regional media.

"The professionals of our scientific community have

concluded that the black bear population in New Jersey exceeds the reasonable carrying capacity of primary habitat to the point where bears now pose a serious life and death threat to the safety and well being of our children. No one of decent conscientiousness would stand idly by and let such irresponsible conditions go unchecked. We implore the professionals of New Jersey wildlife agencies to stand with all caring conservationists demanding a regulated bear hunting season for the state of New Jersey in order to bring the population into healthy check.

"By providing maximum quality outdoor opportunities for the families of New Jersey, by placing tangible value on these precious big-game resources, we will intelligently reduce the threat of maulings and death, while at the same time benefit the balance and health of the wildlife itself.

"Damage control after the fact is always more costly, and in the case of black bears, like with cougars in other states, a human death is a very real probability. This is unacceptable and we implore the powers that be to do the right thing before such a tragedy takes place. The evidence in Ontario, California, Colorado and elsewhere is irrefutable, and must not be ignored before it is too late."

Nugent's efforts do have a positive effect on the non-hunting public, the people who in the long run will decide the fate of bear hunting. So what can you do? That's easy. For starters, you can join the National Rifle Association, a state-level hunting club, the Ted Nugent United Sportsmen of America and the National Bear Hunting Defense Task Force and become one of the unsung heroes of the pro-hunting movement.

The National Bear Hunting Defense Task Force was started in response to House Resolution HR1472, a resolution to ban bear baiting on federal land. The Task Force will fight this and other obnoxious legal maneuverings of the anti-hunters with legal and social expertise.

National Bear Hunting Task Force
C/O U.S. Sportsmen's Alliance
801 Kingsmill Parkway
Columbus, OH 43229-1137
(614) 888-4868

Ted Nugent United Sportsmen of America
4133 West Michigan Ave.
Jackson, MI 49202
(517) 750-9060

National Rifle Association
11250 Waples Mill Rd.
Fairfax, VA 22030
(703) 267-1595

Humans seem to have a love-hate relationship with black bears.

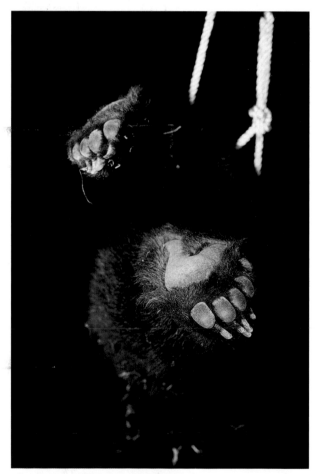

The future of bear hunting is relying on you and me becoming politically active.